Praise for Zach Wahls and

My Two Moms

"[*My Two Moms*] is a wonderful book. You will love it, you will weep at times. It is an incredible demonstration of the power of real values." —Jon Stewart

"[Zach Wahls] lit up the Internet when he delivered a passionate plea to the Iowa House of Representatives in support of gay marriage. Take a look at him . . . a hero." —Ellen DeGeneres

"The most extraordinary thing about his family is its ordinariness and its foundation on that extraordinary substrate called love." —*The Washington Post*

"This book is full of so many practical, often simple, commonsense lessons, quotations, and tips on being a parent, on being a kid— frankly, just being a good person." —*The Huffington Post*

"Few people have such a moving personal tribute to the power of motherhood." —*The Daily Beast*

"Wahls's heart is in the right place. A sincere first effort that aims to chip away at stereotypes surrounding same-sex parents." —*Kirkus Reviews*

"Wahls has a fresh voice, and while still relatively young, his even-handedness and willingness to use his own experiences to address larger social issues is admirable and will likely appeal to all walks of life." —*Publishers Weekly*

"A remarkably engaging, moving story of his experiences, both normal and out of the ordinary. . . . A compelling book that has something for all audiences. All things considered, any reader would be hard-pressed to deny that, if the outcome is any indication, his moms transcended normalcy and did an extraordinary job raising him."

—*Windy City Times*

D0210283

"*My Two Moms* is an engaging portrait of a young man coming of age. With its unthreatening, personable tone and an underpinning of the best kind of persuasive rhetoric, it is the perfect book to act as a bridge between LGBT families and those who aren't so sure about us. Both groups can learn much from it."   —*Bay Windows*

ZEBEDIA WAHLS

Zach Wahls is a bestselling author, speaker, advocate, entrepreneur, Green Bay Packers part-owner, a sixth-generation Iowan, and a commentator on youth- and LGBTQ-related issues. He is the founder and owner of both Iowa City Learns and the Eastern Iowa Renewable Energy Coalition. His writing has appeared in *The Daily Beast, The Des Moines Register, The Daily Iowan, The Huffington Post*, and *Lean Forward*. A video of his heartfelt testimony before the Iowa House Judiciary Committee about his life with two moms was YouTube's most-watched political video of 2011. He lives in Iowa City.

Bruce Littlefield is a bestselling author and journalist whose work has appeared in *The New York Times*, *People*, and *USA Today*. He is also the author of *Moving In: Tales of an Unlicensed Marriage*. He lives in New York.

My Two Moms

Lessons of Love, Strength, and What Makes a Family

∽

Zach Wahls

with

Bruce Littlefield

GOTHAM BOOKS

Twillea—
Thank you so much for bringing
me to campus!

Zach

GOTHAM BOOKS
Published by the Penguin Group
Penguin Group (USA) Inc., 375 Hudson Street,
New York, New York 10014, USA

USA | Canada | UK | Ireland | Australia | New Zealand | India | South Africa | China
Penguin Books Ltd, Registered Offices: 80 Strand, London WC2R 0RL, England

For more information about the Penguin Group visit penguin.com.

Published by Gotham Books, a member of Penguin Group (USA) Inc.

Previously published as a Gotham Books hardcover

First trade paperback printing, April 2013

1 3 5 7 9 10 8 6 4 2

Gotham Books and the skyscraper logo are trademarks of Penguin Group (USA) Inc.

The Library of Congress has catalogued the hardcover edition as follows:
Wahls, Zach.
My two moms : lessons of love, strength, and what makes a family / by Zach Wahls ; with
Bruce Littlefield.
p. cm.
ISBN 978-1-59240-713-2 (HC)   978-1-59240-763-7 (pbk)
1. Wahls, Zach. 2. Children of gay parents—United States
3. Lesbian mothers—United States. 4. Same-sex marriage—United States.
5. Gay rights—United States. I. Littlefield, Bruce (Bruce Duanne) II. Title.
HQ777.8.W34 2012
306.874086'60973—dc23

2011053087

Printed in the United States of America
Set in Sabon • Designed by Elke Sigal

While the author has made every effort to provide accurate telephone numbers and Internet
addresses at the time of publication, neither the publisher nor the author assumes any
responsibility for errors, or for changes that occur after publication. Further, the publisher
does not have any control over and does not assume any responsibility for author or third-
party Web sites or their content.

My Two Moms is not an official publication of the Boy Scouts of America. This publication
is not endorsed by or affiliated with the Boy Scouts of America. Portions of the Scout Oath
excerpted from the official Boy Scouts of America website, www.Scouting.org/FAQ.
Copyright © 2011 Boy Scouts of America. All rights reserved.

---

*Penguin is committed to publishing works of quality and integrity.
In that spirit, we are proud to offer this book to our readers;
however, the story, the experiences, and the words
are the author's alone.*

For Zebby

CONTENTS

❧

Preface

One of my recent lectures brought me back to my birth-place in central Wisconsin. I was slated to speak to students and faculty at each of Mid-State Technical College's three campuses: Wisconsin Rapids, Stevens Point, and Marshfield, my hometown. After the talk in Marshfield, I headed up to Wisconsin Rapids for an interview with a nursing student curious about the best way to interact with same-sex couples and their families when providing medical care in a hospital.

The young woman and I talked for a while. She explained that her brother was gay, and she cared deeply about the comfort and well-being of her patients, but I slowly started to get the sense that she was considerably more religious than she was letting on. About forty-five minutes into the conversation, she disclosed that she was, in her words, a "Jesus freak." However, she went on to explain that she is among a small minority of biblically convicted Christians that believes homosexuality to be a sin, but also recognizes the right of homosexuals to marry a person of the same sex.

I explained my story, how I was conceived, how my moms met, the challenges we faced as a family when my mom Terry was diagnosed with multiple sclerosis—a devastating autoimmune disease that put her in a wheelchair—and the legal obstacles we had to overcome. I talked about their 2009 wedding and how I got to be the best man and give the toast at the reception. She asked questions about how to make families like mine feel comfortable, how to refer to significant others, and slowly she began to share more of her own story.

Amanda had been married two years earlier in a small religious ceremony attended only by herself, her husband, and her pastor. Their union had taken place at the Great Recession's onset, and they could not afford a public ceremony with friends and family. They therefore decided not to file for a marriage license until they could forge their commitment in a public setting. I listened as she explained that in the interim period between their religious ceremony and their public and civic one, she had to check the "single" box on her 1040 form when filing her taxes. "It felt like I was lying," she told me, and then paused. "It hurt."

"Yeah," I said. I understood. "That's what my moms had to do for fifteen years. It's what gay couples all across this country deal with every day."

She looked up at me with clarity in her eyes. "That's wrong," she said softly. Despite being a straight, conservative Christian woman from central Wisconsin, she understood the pain my moms felt.

I nodded, and in that moment I realized that people don't need to be gay or lesbian or bisexual or transgender or have an LGBT parent or parents to know and understand the challenges families like mine are forced to endure.

We just need to listen.

Introduction

First things first: If you're Fred Phelps of the Westboro Baptist Church or Representative Sally homosexuality-is-more-dangerous-than-terrorism Kern,* I suggest you calmly and carefully put this book back on the shelf, as though you never touched it. Hopefully no one around you noticed, and you'll be able to make a clean getaway.

Everyone else, hang with me for a few pages. Yes, even those of you who think my conception was "unnatural" or pity me for my "tragic" upbringing and are convinced that I'm effectively a victim of child abuse. I don't expect my story to convince every one of you that being gay isn't a "choice" or that same-sex marriage should be legal or even that I reached adulthood undamaged by the sexuality of my parents. I promise that I'm not going to ask you to attend a gay wedding and

---

*Yes, she actually said that: http://bit.ly/qj5GV2.

sing show tunes, and I'm not going to try to brainwash you with the "gay agenda." (Although that's probably exactly what I'd say if I were, if there really happened to be some kind of collusion among gays to "convert" people.) No, this is nothing sinister.

What I'd like to do is tell you about my family—my sister, Zebby; my two moms, Jackie and Terry; and our dog, Theodore—and the values my parents instilled in me as I matured into a young man.

In the early 1990s, this country first began a serious, public conversation about same-sex marriage and LGBT rights. Gays were openly entering stable, loving relationships. They were starting families and even raising children through adoption or "artificial" means. Naturally, they wanted to have access to the civil rights, liberties, and protections married straight parents enjoy and use every day to protect their families and loved ones.

But some folks didn't want that.

It was and is a contentious and difficult issue—an issue that has only gotten larger as more and more gay people come out of the closet, settle down, start families, and have kids.

Since the conversation began, a lot has been said and written about the kids being raised in "gay families." (By the way, I find this label silly. My moms don't live in a gay house, drive gay cars, or have a gay dog—as far as we can tell.) But we, the kids of gay parents, haven't really contributed much because we were busy growing up, and adolescence is hard enough as it is without having to respond to society's incessant questions about your family structure. Further, even though there are an estimated two million children of LGBT parents in the United States, of the folks I know raised by openly gay parents, none of us are more than twenty-five years old.

I didn't have to be the kid to write this book. I wasn't trained for this or groomed to be a spokesperson. I was never instructed in the dark arts of subliminal messaging, and I didn't ask to become the subject of national (and, believe it or not, international) media attention because of who my moms are.

I just wanted to defend my family.

Had that defense, my testimony before the Iowa House Judiciary Committee, passed unnoticed or never been submitted in the first place, I never would have been forced to confront the skeptics' questions that came after the committee hearing. I definitely had been asked questions about my parents while growing up, but they were most often aesthetic in nature and largely noninvasive. Usually, those asking were either too polite to intrude or, more often among the inquisitive members of my generation, they figured that having gay parents really wasn't a big deal. As I got older, the questions slowed to a trickle and then stopped almost altogether.

But that changed. After my testimony went viral, conservative bloggers and talk-radio hosts ripped my words apart, offering line-by-line analysis and condescending, often dehumanizing, personal suggestions to "miscreants" and "child-abuse victims" like me.

All this in response to a teenager's six-hundred-word, three-minute speech.

On the evening of Monday, January 31, 2011, I was in Des Moines, Iowa, our state capital, to explain my opposition to

Iowa House Joint Resolution 6—a proposed constitutional amendment that would redefine marriage in our state to be limited to one man and one woman and would also eliminate the possibility of civil unions between same-sex couples in the future. This is a debate still being waged in all fifty states and across much of the world. My testimony touched on my family life, my personal successes, and a few observations I had to offer about growing up with same-sex parents. I had no idea it was going to change my life.

The following morning, the Iowa House Democrats posted a video of my speech on YouTube (without my knowledge). By Friday, it had more than a million hits and had been covered by every major American media outlet except Fox News (shocking, I know). Our whole family had been interviewed on live, national television from my moms' living room, and I was slated to appear on *The Ellen DeGeneres Show* the next week. When asked about the speed with which the video went viral, a YouTube spokesperson told my local newspaper that what had happened was the equivalent of "catching lightning in a bottle," a feat made even more incredible by the fact that I didn't even know I was holding said bottle in the first place.

For reasons I still cannot fully explain—though among them certainly are the facts that I am a straight man, an Iowan, an Eagle Scout, and decently accomplished for my age—I, the medium, became the message, a message that resonated both among those who support the advancement of LGBT rights and those who do not.

So here we are—me writing, you reading—a book that serves as a reply to many of the questions aimed at the kids of gay couples and individuals. But I can't claim to speak for all of us or for the entire gay community. Childhood experiences, whether or not you have same-gender or mixed-gender parents, vary widely. For example, aside from my sister, I'm the only kid I know with gay parents whose biological parent was single at the time of conception. And I don't need to tell you that growing up in Iowa City, Iowa, is different from growing up in Greenwich Village. This is the story of only one family—though I hope this inspires other kids to share their stories—and the thoughts and recollections of only one person.

This book is an exploration of the values my moms taught me, values driven home by my journey to Eagle Scout—the Boy Scouts of America's highest rank—and how they pertain to the questions folks have for kids like me.

It is a response to all those who say I am "different."

While this is a reality I was at first hesitant to acknowledge, ultimately, there is no doubt that I have always been different. Folks from all walks of life have been informing and reminding me of this difference since I was a young child, and they continue to do so today. But it is on rare occasion that they explicitly define what this difference is, and I suspect the hesitancy to do so is the result of a culture that by and large craves conformity whenever possible and finds comfort in its largely homogenous nature.

I am different insofar as I am defined by a number of traits I do not share with the majority of my peers. Among many things, I am the son of a same-sex couple, was conceived using assistive reproductive technology, and scored in the 99th percentile of the ACT. I am also an Eagle Scout, a small-business owner, a Unitarian Universalist, and a state championship–winning debater.

My family, too, is undeniably different from the American mean. Two moms is a familial construct that was considered novel until only recently, though it is still disparaged as invalid by a shrinking—though increasingly shrill—minority. That minority would have you believe that this difference is all defining, that it disqualifies my mothers from access to civil marriage (though the Iowa constitution would beg to differ), and that it renders my family undeserving of all the rights, privileges, and protections enjoyed every day by "straight" families.

Yet my moms' same-sex relationship is just one difference among many that are found in families of all shapes and sizes.

At a young age, my family experienced the cruel reality of a chronic autoimmune disease. My mom Terry was diagnosed with multiple sclerosis at the age of forty-four, a development that, at nine years old, I could not even begin to understand. And, as a result, there is another significant difference between the Reger-Wahls household and the rest of America: After twelve years of struggling with multiple sclerosis, the one treatment that has worked for my mom is a radical change to her diet, so you'll find no gluten-based foods in our cupboards and no dairy products in our refrigerator. Though—and don't mention this to her—you'll find plenty of both at my apartment.

Yes, I can certainly see my family's differences—and I can acknowledge my own—but I must confess, however, that I am unable to actually *feel* those differences. I have, after all, no control group against which I may compare the experiences of my life, no memories of a more "normal," one-mom-and-one-dad past against which to weigh the present. Though society regularly informs me that my family structure is different, I feel as though I'm being told that I am wearing different colored socks. Yes, you might not like how they look, but beyond inciting the occasional bout of aesthetic displeasure, how does it affect your life?

I know mixing socks is purely a visual example. Being raised by a lesbian couple is substantively different from being raised by a straight, mixed-gender couple. But I suspect you would find yourself incapable of discerning either the sex of my parents or color of my socks from simply shaking my hand and having a conversation over coffee. In fact, to date, not once have I ever been confronted by an individual who realized independently that I was raised by a gay couple. Not once. And I'll be surprised if that changes over the next twenty.

But besides the obvious, what were these substantive differences? Well, I learned how to shave from my best friend's dad and how to tie a tie from an article in *Playboy*. I had to carefully explain to an Indian visa officer that I left the "Name of Father" space blank on my visa application because I don't know it—I've never met the man, nor do I plan to. The sexuality of my parents, and the rejection they felt from the Christian faith in which they were both raised, led them to embrace the more accepting teachings of Unitarian Universalism, another meaningful and substantive difference from the American mean.

Yet when I declared before the Iowa House Judiciary Committee during that hearing on House Joint Resolution 6, that "the sexuality of my parents has had zero effect on the content of my character," I was not bearing falsehood. I believe this with all my heart to be true. After all, one's sexuality does not determine a person's response to discrimination. That response is informed not by the color of your skin, your gender identity, your sexuality, or any other immutable characteristic, but by the beliefs you hold and the values you prize—*the content of your character.*

Much has changed since my testimony before the Iowa House of Representatives and the viral aftermath that followed in its wake, and there are still days when I have a hard time believing this is all real. As I received invitations to speak at political events and fund-raisers, in classrooms and boardrooms, I couldn't help but ask myself, what could I, then still too young to order a beer, possibly have to say that you don't already know? But as I've traveled around my state and across the country, folks who were once on the fence or downright opposed to LGBT rights have told me that my story has changed their minds. In the years following, I've realized my experience has a resonance—a relevance—I had completely failed to understand.

And while this tale could begin in any number of places—our family's move from Wisconsin to Iowa, my mom Terry breaking up with her longtime girlfriend, the legalization of same-sex marriage in Iowa, the day I ran home from kindergarten to tell my moms I wanted to join the Cub Scouts—the journey upon which I have most recently embarked has a clear starting point. The chairman of the Iowa House Judiciary Committee called out my name, I took a deep breath, and then I stepped forward to a lectern in the Iowa House of

Representatives to defend my family and the marriage of my two moms.

> *Good evening, Mr. Chairman. My name is Zach Wahls. I'm a sixth-generation Iowan and an engineering student at the University of Iowa, and I was raised by two women.*

CHAPTER 1

"Be Prepared"

Mine has always been a sit-down-and-have-dinner kind of family. So when I announced at a Sunday night supper that I was preparing to testify the following night at a state hearing on gay marriage, the four of us launched into a hearty conversation on the topic. Zebby, my then sixteen-year-old sister, was still shocked that anyone could possibly be opposed to the union our parents shared. Jackie, my non-biological mom (also known as "Short Mom"), wanted to know who would be there and how many people might show up, her protective den mother instincts kicking in. Terry, my biological mom (or "Tall Mom"), was eager to hear the remarks I had written so she could help me fine-tune them.

My moms always used our dinner-table conversations as a way to prepare my sister and me for the daily challenges of life. From simple reminders to do our homework and practice the piano to the more complex task of teaching us how to deal with a school bully, these nightly dialogues were both a safe harbor and a staging ground.

It was around the dinner table that they introduced us to the book *Teaching Your Children Values* by Linda and Richard Eyre, which gives parents a yearlong, month-by-month plan for teaching their children values, such as self-discipline, perseverance, kindness, and honesty. Every night since I was a young child, we'd share examples of that month's value. Although I'd usually just toss out a quick example en route to whatever was on my plate, over the course of nearly two decades, these moral explorations sank in. My moms equipped me with a strong sense of right and wrong and taught me that the world is rarely black and white.

It was around the dinner table that they carefully informed us of Terry's multiple sclerosis diagnosis. They explained why she had been falling down so frequently and why she would sometimes spend entire days in the master bedroom, paralyzed by pain. They walked my sister and me through what this development would mean for our family's future. They described the differences we might start to see as her MS progressed, and they delicately revealed that there was no cure.

It was around the dinner table that they prepared me for my Eagle Scout board of review, the final step a young man takes on his way to the highest honor the Boy Scouts of America has to offer. Jackie asked me questions about the history of Scouts and what the symbolism of the badges, patches, and ranks were. Terry tested my knowledge of the Scout motto, law, oath, and slogan. I could rattle off these precepts forward, backward, and while patting my head and rubbing my stomach.

The Scout motto: Be prepared.

The Scout law: A Scout is trustworthy, loyal,
helpful, friendly, courteous, kind, obedient,
cheerful, thrifty, brave, clean, and reverent.

The Scout oath: On my honor I will do my best to
do my duty to God and my country and to obey
the Scout law; to help other people at all times; to
keep myself physically strong, mentally awake,
and morally straight.

The Scout slogan: Do a good turn daily.

And so it was appropriate that, once again, we found ourselves sitting around the dinner table, discussing the testimony I'd be delivering the following evening to defend
marriage equality before the Iowa Legislature. As excited and
intrigued as we all were, none of us could have predicted what
would happen next.

"Wait a minute," Jackie said. "The hearing's tomorrow?
And you started writing your testimony yesterday?"

"Yeaaaah," I replied in a long drawl, my trademarked
I'm-not-as-ready-as-I-should-be smile plastered across my
face.

"So much for 'being prepared,'" she said with a laugh.

She didn't know the half of it.

I'd only found out about the hearing a few days before it
was slated to take place. I actually wound up scrapping the
version I presented to my family that night almost completely
and worked into the wee hours of the morning preparing a

new draft. Over the course of about ten hours, I had gone through four vastly different takes, each one focused on an entirely separate part of the same-sex marriage debate, before settling on the aspect I knew best: my family. Satisfied, I printed the final draft and called it a night.

The following morning, as I stood in front of the mirror and pulled my tie snug, the motto of the Boy Scouts ricocheted through my mind: "Be prepared. Be prepared. Be prepared," as though, for some reason, I wasn't. But I had worked hard to pull my testimony together at a moment's notice. And in some ways, it felt like my entire life had been lived in preparation for the day's events. Glancing back in the mirror, I double-checked my suit—I wouldn't have time to come back to my apartment before leaving for Des Moines after the day's classes.

I knew the people I'd face at the hearing—particularly those on the "other side"—would be judging more than my words. They'd be looking at every square inch of my appearance and examining every aspect of my demeanor, hoping to spot a stray sign that my parents hadn't raised me right, as though their "lesbian parenting" would manifest itself as some sort of telltale physical defect. The kids of heterosexual parents at the hearing would not endure such scrutiny.

Not even close.

It was on that last night of January 2011 that I climbed into my well-worn Pontiac Grand Am and drove off to Des Moines, utterly unaware of the journey that lay ahead.

I plugged in my iPod and cued up Kanye West's latest album. On my Speech and Debate team in high school, I had discovered that the best way to know if you have something down is to try to recite it while listening to music. And that's how I practiced my speech as I made my way to Iowa's capital, mumbling the words that were—unbeknownst to me—about to change the course of my life.

I pulled off I-235 West onto East 15th Street in Des Moines. In the gray distance, through the snowflakes, I could see the gold dome perched atop the Iowa capitol, glowing with a pale shine against the dark night sky. I found a parking spot and made my way toward what I knew would soon become a rhetorical firefight, but I was largely unperturbed. As a state-champion high school debater, it is a rare instance when I take an argument personally. As the son of a married lesbian couple, I had developed thick skin and quick reflexes.

I was ready to defend my moms.

To put it mildly, gay marriage is a contentious issue. It tends to engender passionate responses from just about everyone and often provokes the worst in all of us. For those seeking marriage equality, easy accusations of bigotry, ignorance, and homophobia fly without remorse. The traditional marriage advocates are quick to label their opponents as godless sodomites seeking to advance the "gay agenda." Or something like that. But reality isn't so simple. The fact is that the conversation from both sides is driven by fear: fear of social and legal disenfranchisement on the one hand, and of the loss of religious tradition and an assault on normalcy on the other.

As I stood beneath the rotunda in the Iowa capitol, stumbling through muted rehearsals of my testimony, the significance of the night had not yet sunk in. With dozens more speakers present than would be able to have the floor for three precious minutes apiece during the two-hour legislative hearing, I realized my testimony might not even be heard. I chatted with other marriage equality supporters, while anxiously waiting for my name to be called.

When it was announced that I would be the fourth speaker, I walked through the doors of the Iowa House chamber and into a standing-room-only crowd. Immediately I noticed the TV cameras, which were all pointed at the speaker's lectern. I hadn't realized that our speeches were going to be recorded. *Of course they are*, I thought. *This is a hearing on gay marriage. What were you expecting?*

Certainly not that.

The only other time I had visited the capitol was for an elementary school field trip, and back then the room had been empty. Now, a college student, I could see that it was far larger than I remembered. And tonight it was filled with people and an energy that can only be described as unbridled and unpredictable.

Knowing I'd be speaking shortly, I took a spot and stood against the wall. After about ten minutes of opening remarks from the Iowa House Judiciary Committee chairman, Richard Anderson, the state lawmakers in attendance introduced themselves.

I was taken aback by how many political figures were present. Had I known there would be so many legislators in attendance, I would have, I don't know, shined my shoes or something. I suddenly realized I was more nervous than I had thought.

When my name was announced, I walked toward the lectern, turning to face the room. All eyes were on me. My hands were shaking as I took a deep breath, tapped the start button on the timer of my iPod Touch, and set it down. I had three minutes to make my case.

> *Good evening, Mr. Chairman. My name is Zach Wahls. I'm a sixth-generation Iowan and an engineering student at the University of Iowa, and I was raised by two women.*
>
> *My biological mom, Terry, told her parents that she was pregnant, that the artificial insemination had worked, and they wouldn't even acknowledge it. It actually wasn't until I was born and they succumbed to my infantile cuteness that they broke down and told her that they were thrilled to have another grandson. Unfortunately, neither of them lived to see her marry her partner, Jackie, of fifteen years when they wed in 2009. My younger sister and only sibling was born in 1994. We actually have the same anonymous donor, so we're full siblings, which is really cool for me.*
>
> *I guess the point is that our family really isn't so different from any other Iowa family. When I'm home, we go to church together. We eat dinner. We go on vacations. But, you know, we have our hard times, too; we get in fights. Actually, my mom Terry was diagnosed with multiple sclerosis in 2000. It is a devastating disease that put her in a wheelchair, so we've had our struggles. But, you know, we're Iowans. We don't expect anyone to solve our problems for us. We'll fight our own battles. We just hope for equal and fair treatment from our government.*

*Being a student at the University of Iowa, the
topic of same-sex marriage comes up quite frequently
in classroom discussions. You know, the question always comes down to, "Well, can gays even raise
kids?" And the conversation gets quiet for a moment,
because most people don't really have an answer.
And then I raise my hand and say, "Actually, I was
raised by a gay couple, and I'm doing pretty well."*

*I scored in the ninety-ninth percentile on the ACT.
I'm actually an Eagle Scout. I own and operate my
own small business. If I was your son, Mr. Chairman, I believe I'd make you very proud. I'm not
really so different from any of your children. My family really isn't so different from yours. After all, your
family doesn't derive its sense of worth from being
told by the state, "You're married, congratulations!"
No, the sense of family comes from the commitment
we make to each other to work through the hard
times so we can enjoy the good ones. It comes from
the love that binds us.*

That's what makes a family.

*So what you're voting here isn't to change us. It's
not to change our families. It's to change how the law
views us, how the law treats us. You are voting for
the first time in the history of our state to codify discrimination into our constitution, a constitution that
but for the proposed amendment is the least amended
constitution in the United States of America.*

*You are telling Iowans that "some among you are
second-class citizens who do not have the right to*

marry the person you love." So, will this vote affect my family? Would it affect yours?

Over the next two hours, I'm sure we're going to hear plenty of testimony about how damaging having gay parents is on kids. But in my nineteen years, not once have I ever been confronted by an individual who realized independently that I was raised by a gay couple.

And you know why?

Because the sexual orientation of my parents has had zero effect on the content of my character. Thank you very much.

I think I remember the crowd cheering as I walked back to my spot against the wall, a vague memory confirmed later by video evidence. I am certain I was sweating. Thank God I decided to wear a suit jacket.

Three nights later, our family was once again huddled around the dinner table. But instead of eating dinner, we were trying to figure out what the camera crew setting up in our living room wanted us to wear. We were an hour away from a live interview on national television, and, needless to say, none of us really knew what we were doing.

We had gone through a lot together in our life as a family, successfully navigating the grueling trials of multiple sclerosis, legal challenges, and social discrimination, and we had learned a lot along the way. We were prepared for a lot of things.

But we weren't prepared for this—not even close.

As soon as the interview was over, a cell phone rang. It was Jackie's mom, Grandma Esther, a graying Catholic woman living in central Wisconsin, and she skipped hello to get right to her point. She demanded to know why I had referred to Jackie, her daughter, as "Mom." Jackie was at our kitchen table holding her cell phone to her ear, still dressed in a freshly pressed shirt and slacks, and I watched as she struggled to maintain her composure.

Guilt flooded my mind.

I had insisted that the interview be of the whole family, not just me. Despite Jackie's shyness—something most people forget about after they've gotten to know her—she had begrudgingly agreed to take part. Now she was being forced to explain to her own mother why I, her son, would refer to her as "Mom." I wanted to interject that Esther had never questioned Zebby or me when we called her Grandma, but instead, feeling the tension of the call, I stayed silent.

I was engulfed in emotion, unsure what to do, so I just stood in our living room as the camera crew went about disassembling their lighting rig. Abruptly, Jackie flipped her phone shut. The conversation was over. I walked over to the table and looked at her. There were no tears in her eyes, but I could feel the defeat in her heart. She looked up, and with a knowing nod, I wrapped her in a hug.

This should have been a celebration, a moment of triumph. But even as we stood in the afterglow of the preceding forty-eight hours—amid the pride and love both of my moms had felt as my defense of our family had been played over and over again on national TV—all I could feel was that as far as we've come, we still have a long way to go.

CHAPTER 2

Obedient

When I was young, we would visit Grandma Lois's house in northeastern Iowa. Terry's mom always had quite a collection of board games for us to play. As soon as we'd get to her house, I'd give her a kiss and then head right to her hallway closet to dig through the assortment of colorful boxes stacked in it. There were, of course, the usual suspects, like Monopoly, Scrabble, and Chinese checkers, but there was also my personal favorite, Life. I think Life was Grandma's favorite, too, as she played it with Zebby and me almost every time we visited.

The game reproduces a person's travels through life, from college to retirement, with jobs, marriage, and maybe even children along the way. I think one of the reasons I liked the game of Life so much was that in it you get to grow up, and when I was a kid, I always wanted to grow up. In addition, there are three things that separate the game of Life from other board games. First, the board has small mountains, buildings, and other three-dimensional objects. Second, there's the spinning wheel, which whirls around like the one on *Wheel of Fortune*—Grandma Lois's favorite show. Third, the playing pieces are tiny plastic cars in a variety of colors, each with six holes in the top to accommodate the blue and pink "people pegs" that are placed in the car throughout the game as each player gets married and has or adopts children.

During one of our first games—I must have been around seven years old, definitely before sex had ever crossed my mind—we were playing and I "got married." I put a blue peg in the passenger's seat of my game piece next to my own blue piece.

Grandma Lois glanced at me with what I now recognize as a quizzical look.

"Are you sure that's what you want to do?" she asked.

"Yep," I said, confidently. My best friends were all boys. Duh.

"Well," she said, taking a thoughtful pause. "I guess there isn't any rule against it."

"Why would there be a rule against it?" I asked.

Grandma Lois just smiled. Though I didn't always pick a blue peg and Zebby didn't always pick a pink peg, Grandma Lois always happily rode through Life with a blue peg at her side and fond memories of her deceased husband, John, in her heart.

In the game of Life, she could pick whomever she wanted to ride next to her.

Years earlier, when Terry had told her parents that she was looking into artificial insemination, they immediately told her it was a horrible idea. Having grown up as a fifth-generation farmer's daughter in rural Iowa, she knew her parents wouldn't be jumping up and down with joy, but she hadn't anticipated their utter disdain and how vehemently they opposed the idea. Her mother went so far as to tell Terry that she would not only be putting her career in jeopardy but also that society would never accept the child of a lesbian mom. Her dad ended what she describes as a "jarringly memorable" conversation by telling her, "You're out of your goddamned mind."

But Terry Wahls had always been one to give her parents her opinion and had a habit of standing her ground when she knew she was right. At the age of nine she'd protested her father's decision to label their farm "John Wahls and Sons." Such a naming pattern was the typical farming convention of the time, but Terry thought "John Wahls and Family" was more appropriate. After all, if she was going to be getting up at five every morning to work on the farm—not to mention the ceaseless efforts of her mother—the name of their farm ought to reflect that. Grandpa John gave it some thought, and despite his initial reservations, begrudgingly agreed that "John Wahls and Family" was indeed more appropriate—but he refused to adopt the alternative name, holding fast to society's convention.

This time around, however, she was less confident in her convictions. What if her dad was right and she was out of her mind? It wasn't until she had the chance to discuss her conundrum with some other family members that she fully made up her mind to move forward. She was having a pizza dinner with her aunt Cora; Cora's sixteen-year-old daughter, Shannon; and a few of Shannon's high school friends. The girls told Terry that they didn't think it would be a big deal for a kid to have a lesbian mom, and (fortunately for my sister and me) Terry believed them.

My mom has been telling me the story of how I came to be since I first started nursing. I was born under atypical circumstances, after a series of somewhat spectacular events and what amounted to an act of civil disobedience. It took a failed in vitro fertilization (IVF) cycle and a few unsuccessful attempts at artificial insemination (AI) before the fertility efforts finally took, and a single, thirty-four-year-old lesbian physician living in conservative central Wisconsin in 1990 became pregnant.

Got all that?

Like so many other women, Terry Wahls had always imagined herself as a mother. She wanted to experience the joys and trials of raising a child and all the life-enriching experiences that accompany motherhood. But she was a single gay woman, and society told her no at nearly every turn, making her journey to parenthood not just difficult, but practically impossible.

In the late 1980s, Terry was working as an internal medicine physician in Marshfield, Wisconsin, and dating another female physician. When Terry shared her hopes of having children, the woman she was dating made it clear that she didn't share those dreams and promptly broke up with Terry. For the next several years Terry privately struggled with the thought of becoming a mom, wondering if she could raise a child as a single parent and, if she could, if that child would be okay with a lesbian mother. There were, after all, no guarantees. Further, if she did decide to have a child, how exactly would she go about it? As a doctor, she knew that the ticking biological clock wasn't just a metaphor. The longer she waited, the lower the likelihood that she'd be able to get pregnant. She's told me that she finally realized it wasn't about making the right decision; it was about making a decision and living with—and learning from—the consequences.

Terry made an appointment with her friend Bruce, the fertility expert in her clinic, and considered herself lucky to be a doctor with partners who would help her. But, after getting a sperm donor catalog, Terry got bad news. Her ultrasound, which had been intended to check if her eggs were ready for insemination, ended up revealing an ovarian mass that would have to be surgically removed before she would be able to get pregnant. Her inner physician feared the growth might be cancer, but it turned out to be a cyst and "full of blood," as I remember her telling me. Terry didn't have cancer. She had severe endometriosis, which was completely clogging her fallopian tubes. This meant that any attempts with artificial insemination would be highly unlikely to succeed—perhaps impossible. It's interesting, and perhaps significant, to note that even if Terry had been straight and married to a man, she still wouldn't have been able to get pregnant by the "natural" method. Without reproductive technologies—like IVF or AI—she would never have been a mother, regardless of her sexual orientation.

Terry began to wonder if her mother was right. Maybe she should just give up trying to get pregnant.

The last remaining option would be IVF. The procedure would require daily doctor visits for ultrasounds and lab draws for a couple of weeks at a time. Since the clinic where she worked didn't have an IVF center, Terry looked for a year to find an IVF clinic to enroll in. Bruce suggested the University of Wisconsin–Madison, which she considered feasible because it was only two and a half hours away. When she called a doctor at the clinic, he was initially very friendly, talking in a collaborative doctor-to-doctor manner. He told her that they had great success rates for women with severe endometriosis. Then, he asked, "What is the problem with your husband that requires the use of donor sperm? Maybe we have a way around that for you." When she replied that she would be doing this as a single parent, his tone switched from warm and fuzzy to cold and icy. He abruptly said, "We do not *do* illegitimate children in our clinic," and hung up the phone without waiting for a reply.

Terry couldn't find any IVF clinics in the Midwest that would accept a single woman—to say nothing of the fact that she was gay. Months later, at a Women in Medicine conference, Terry recounted the doctor's rude comments to her colleagues. The female doctors at the seminar were outraged, and one of them, a physician at the University of California, San Francisco, vowed she would get Terry into the IVF program there.

Now that she had a clinic, all Terry had to do was pick a sperm donor.

She still laughs every time she describes how pitiful the sperm donor catalog for humans was compared to the elaborate breeder catalogs for prizewinning bulls that her dad received during her childhood on the farm. Those catalogs included glossy, color photographs of the bull, and along with the bull's name were listed its pedigree, trophies, awards, statistics for its offspring, and the name of the farmer. The human sperm donor list included no such photographs, no pedigrees, and since it was listing anonymous donors, no names.

All Terry had to do was answer a series of questions about the traits she'd prefer in a potential donor, such as skin color and complexion, eye color, hair color, height, weight, and education level. Straight couples usually try to match the sperm donor's characteristics to those of the husband, but that wasn't an issue for Terry. She didn't really care if the donor's hair was blond or black, curly or straight. She just wanted the donor to have completed at least two years of college and be tall. Not just because she was tall herself, but she strategically thought that if her children might face bullying because of their mother's sexuality, a couple extra inches might be helpful.

She received a list of donors who met her criteria, but all she had to base her final decision on was two basic biographical lines about each guy. She picked donor number 1033, a six-foot-five fellow studying to be a tax attorney, who also said he played basketball and classical piano. Though Terry knew it was still a long shot, she began giving herself the necessary hormone injections in her buttocks twice a day. When she arrived in San Francisco, everything seemed to be going well. Doctors told her that the ultrasound looked good, and she was producing plenty of estrogen.

On Halloween morning in 1990, she walked to the clinic

through San Francisco's Castro district and its sea of gay men in various entertaining costumes—including drag queens, lots of leather, and one Native American whom she remembers "looked like he escaped from the Village People." But when she arrived at the clinic, she got more bad news. The doctors told her that her ovaries had fizzled out. She only had two, maybe three, eggs ready to go. It was not enough to harvest and do the IVF, so they canceled the cycle but let her have the donor's sperm through a plain, old-fashioned turkey-baster insemination. Given the scarring on her fallopian tubes, it was the mother of all long shots. (No pun intended.) After, she had dinner with friends and flew back to Wisconsin.

The night Terry got home, she wrote in her journal that it was time to give up on the dream of having kids. She was so certain her chance of getting pregnant was zero that she didn't even bother to get a pregnancy test.

And then a miracle happened. One of 1033's sperm had fought its way through her collapsed fallopian tubes and found a way to unite with one of those two viable eggs.

Terry Wahls, the single lesbian physician from rural Iowa now transplanted to central Wisconsin, was pregnant.

She immediately called her parents to share the news. "I'm pregnant, Dad," she said into the phone as she sat alone at her kitchen counter. "I'm gonna be a mom."

Terry wanted her father to say something—anything. But there was nothing, just the empty space of stunned silence. "Didn't you hear me, Dad? I'm pregnant."

And then finally her dad asked, "Well, have you heard that the price of corn is inching up?"

I think it says something about Iowans that, when uncomfortable, our go-to conversation topic isn't the weather: it's the price of corn.

I was born July 15, 1991. I was named Zacharia, because my mom believes strong names begin with a "Z," and Zacharia was a professional-sounding name that also had a "rather pleasant nickname." Like most of Terry Wahls's decisions, this one was deliberate and well thought out. And thank God, because the other name she liked was Wolfgang.

When Terry returned home from the hospital with me, she checked the local newspaper for my birth announcement. There wasn't one. She presumed that the hospital had not provided the information to the newspaper, so she called the Labor and Delivery suite. "Dr. Wahls," they said, "didn't you know, the paper won't print any announcements for single mothers?" She was appalled. How could the paper refuse to print public information? She thought that perhaps it wasn't really the paper, but more likely the Catholic hospital trying to interject its religious values into the world.

She called the newspaper, and after talking to a few people, she finally got the editor on the phone. "We put in announcements for all sorts of things," he told her, his tone impatient and bothered. "The price depends on the size of your announcement."

"What?" she asked. "How can our newspaper refuse to publish my son's birth announcement?"

"Don't act surprised," he said. "I know you've already been told that we only announce *legitimate* children." Wincing, she noted that word again, which implied questions of validity, of worth and meaning. She let the editor know that she didn't understand how printing her name and her son's name, both a matter of public record, could be a problem for the newspaper. The editor informed her that the paper would be taking a legal risk by printing anything unless they knew the woman was married, because of "potential problems in regard to proving paternity" and "to protect the interests of the child." Unable to believe what she was hearing, my mom promptly notified him that she would be speaking with her attorney and hung up.

She was still stewing, pondering the best course of action, when she received a call from the same editor, whose voice sounded decidedly different from their first call. Even over the phone, she could tell he was nervous by the anxious tempo of his speech. "You were correct, of course, Dr. Wahls," he told her. "Because you did not want to name the father, we can announce your son's birth. Unfortunately, we've already missed today's paper, but we'll get him into Friday's paper."

Though thrilled, Terry Wahls didn't stop with her own personal satisfaction. She asked the editor if this meant the paper was changing its policy. He tried to avoid her question, instead asking about the correct spelling of my name and my grandparents' names.

She repeated the question.

He told her that the corporate owners of the newspaper had to be involved in any policy changes, which would take time. Couldn't he simply put her son's name in the paper? Wouldn't that make her happy? But Terry's never been one for special treatment and quickly told him that she would be more than happy to pay for an attorney to advocate for all single moms who did not get their birth announcements in the paper.

That did it. The policy was changed, both by the paper and Saint Joseph's Hospital. As my mom later discovered, the hospital did indeed have an unwritten policy that said it would not release information concerning births by unwed mothers.

That Friday, for the first time in Marshfield's history, a single mother and her son made the paper: "Terry Lynn Wahls 'Mom' and Zacharia Patrick Wahls 'Zach' proudly announce Zach's birth at 9:26 pm on Monday, July 15, 1991." In addition to the birth announcement, there was an added bonus. My mom had changed the paper's procedures. Though I was too busy crying and nursing to enjoy the victory, it was a happy moment. The headline on the editorial page read: "Unwed births now accepted," and the article began: "Society is changing, and our policies are changing with it," a political reality that, over the ensuing two decades, would manifest itself in more ways than Terry, and most members of the LGBT community, ever imagined.

My mom sent my birth announcement and the editorial to Aunt Cora, with a note that said, "Here in Marshfield, the world is changing. And you know what? I can hear the cheering. It is coming from lots of people. My mom was wrong. There are plenty of people who think it is OK."

As I grew up, I'd discover there were also plenty of people who thought it wasn't.

THE MERITS OF OBEDIENCE

When my mom sees something wrong, she has always been willing to fight to have it fixed—even if other people think she's just being a pain in the ass. She's a living example of how to change rules when the rules are unfair. Such ability requires a strong sense of right and wrong, the capacity to carefully work through a problem, and the sheer will to keep going when you are rejected and denied at every possible turn.

She's taught me that, for things that matter, there are times when you have to buck conventional wisdom and question tradition that exists only for tradition's sake. This isn't to say that you have to disobey the law or try to radically redefine the world—it's to say that obedience and respect are both good when you are obeying something for the right reasons.

In the 1990s, conventional wisdom said that single, lesbian women couldn't be mothers. Conventional wisdom said that unwed women had illegitimate children. At other times, in other places, people were told by conventional wisdom that the color of one's skin made slavery okay, that wives were property of their husbands, that marriages were arranged, and that the sun orbited the earth. Although the wisdom of the crowd is important and the lessons of tradition are valuable, ultimately we are each responsible for our own decisions and must make our own judgments on what is right and what is wrong and act accordingly.

This was a sentiment echoed by my time in the Scouts, which taught us that even though a Scout should obey the rules and laws of his community, country, family, school, and troop, "if he thinks these rules and laws are unfair, he tries to have them changed in an orderly manner rather than disobeying them."

And this is true of my mom. While she was swimming against the current trying to get pregnant with me, she didn't stop obeying the speed limit or paying her taxes in protest. She still believed in the value of regimented discipline, maintained a strict exercise program, and was not about to let me be a slacker. As I grew up, the lessons she had learned from her parents while growing up on that small farm in rural Iowa were passed on to me. I did my homework, kept up on my chores, was in at curfew, and limited my gaming time to less than an hour a day (most of the time).

Trust me, I didn't need a dad to teach me obedience.

One evening after my mom got home from work, we were taking a walk around our neighborhood. Terry was pushing Zebby in her stroller, and I was bouncing around them and singing a nonsensical song I had made up. I had just lost my front tooth and had money in my pocket from my new best friend, the Tooth Fairy. One of the lines was something like,

"Oh, how fun it is to be a fairy . . ." I didn't know that the word "fairy," in its modern context, is often used as a derogatory term for being a gay man. At that age, I didn't really even know what "gay" was. I was just happily singing about a fairy, and my mom stopped me in the street and said, "Hey, Zach, you can't say that."

I was confused. "Why?" I asked. "What's wrong with being a fairy?"

I was too young for her to explain the euphemism to me. "Zach," she said with a smile. "You just don't want to call yourself a fairy. All right?" I was very respectful of her wisdom, so I simply took her word for it. Obeying her request, I changed my tune.

The because-I-said-so line is occasionally acceptable when the parent—or any other authority figure—has meritorious explanations at other times. By demonstrating a thoughtful decision-making process about what I was and was not allowed to do, my moms built a strong, trusting relationship, making obedience easy.

"Because I said so," on the other hand, is a poor legal explanation for anything. But, fundamentally, it is the core legal argument beneath the "sanctity of marriage." Britney Spears's fifty-five-hour marriage and Kim Kardashian's seventy-two-day marriage both uphold the "sanctity of marriage," but my moms' sixteen-year commitment doesn't?

Why?

"Because I said so."

CHAPTER 3

◈

Trustworthy

On December 21, 1996, Terry Lynn Wahls took the hand of Jacqueline Kay Reger and made public, openly and honestly, the highest commitment two loving people can make. They said, "I do."

Jackie and Terry made it "official" by walking hand in hand down the aisle at our church to the theme song of *Star Trek: Voyager.* They exchanged vows before our minister and God and declared in front of friends and family the commitment of their relationship.

It is a commitment that has endured much adversity.

To say that Jackie wound up running our family as a single parent is a stretch, but at times it would not have been far from the truth. I sometimes wondered if Jackie, when she first met Terry, had known what was around the corner, if she would have turned on her heels (not that she ever wore heels) and run in the other direction. But I never asked her. I didn't need to. As I watched Jackie day after day, I witnessed first-hand what "commitment" means.

She kept her promise.

Jackie has always said that she noticed my mom before she met her. At just an inch shy of six feet, Terry is hard to miss. But what Jackie really remembers about the night they met at a coffeehouse is that Terry sat down immediately to her right and smiled and nodded as Jackie told her about her life in Wausau and her work on her master's in nursing. It might have been called love at first sight had Terry not turned away during Jackie's soliloquy. Terry's hearing, as Jackie later discovered, isn't the best, and with the music in the room, she couldn't hear a thing Jackie was saying. So after attempting to listen for a while, my mom eventually decided it was probably best to just turn around and enjoy the music.

I'm not sure where I got my skills with the ladies, but they sure aren't from her.

Still, before Terry left that night, Jackie had taken my mom's telephone number. A few years later, when Jackie was assigned to find lesbians to participate in a breast cancer screening study, Nurse Jackie decided she'd call Dr. Wahls, "*the* lesbian physician in Marshfield," to see if she knew anyone who might take part. It was during a follow-up conversation that the newly single Terry suggested an afternoon at Discovery Zone with her two kids—a non-date. Terry had just gone through a bad breakup— the result of the fertility drug–fueled roller coaster of mental states she rode while trying to get pregnant with my sister, Zebby—and arrived at the conclusion that she was probably going to raise her two children as a single mom.

Jackie knew something about bad breakups.

She told Terry that a woman she had been with for five years had broken her heart. When Jackie discovered that the woman was having an affair, their trust was broken, and their relationship was over. Jackie, who had been a second mother to the woman's four kids, had been shown the door and shut out of their lives.

Ten years before that, Jackie had been engaged to a young man. A few months into the engagement, however, after some serious soul-searching, she decided that if she couldn't be honest with her friends and family about her sexuality, she had to at least be honest with herself. She broke off the engagement, hoping she hadn't broken his heart but knowing she had done what was right for both of them.

Terry told Jackie the story of donor number 1033 and how, when I was six weeks old, she had visited her doctor for a post-partum checkup and decided she'd like to try getting pregnant again. Besides being really happy to be a mother, she wanted me to have a sibling. Bruce, one of her partners at the clinic, suggested she order sperm from the same donor, so her children would have the same biological father, and then keep the liquid vials on ice until she was ready.

She went through hormone treatments that wrecked both her emotions and a relationship, but on the tenth and last vial left from donor 1033, my mom got pregnant with twins. One of them died at fourteen weeks, and she herself almost died while delivering. The last thing she remembers thinking in labor was, "Zach will be an orphan." When the fog lifted, she realized she hadn't died. I wasn't an orphan, and I had a baby sister.

———

From the start of their non-relationship, both of my moms made clear to the other that honesty would be at the foundation of whatever relationship might develop. Over the course of a few weeks, Terry went through a lengthy back-and-forth debate with herself about whether she really wanted to risk being involved with someone. She had come to peace with a future that included only her, Zeb, and me, convincing herself that her heart would be fine with being single. But she was unable to shake the lingering thought that there was something special about Jackie Reger, the cute nurse from Wausau, Wisconsin.

One Saturday night, Jackie knocked on the door of our simple ranch-style house in Marshfield and joined us for our first dinner together. After we ate, I biked around the family room in our basement on my tricycle, and Jackie told Terry what a good mom she thought she was. Terry said she was incredibly blessed, and as she watched me pedal said, "I never would have thought I could love a man so much."

That night, Jackie slept on the spare bed in my room. Terry camped out in her room with Zebby and me, debating with herself about the trajectory of her life. She was thinking about us. She thought Zebby and I were now old enough that there should be no more casual dating. She was going to have a serious relationship, or none at all.

The following morning, my mom held Zebby in her arms, and we stood on our porch and waved as Jackie drove off. The relationship had ended before it began. Later that day, my mom called Jackie to apologize and said she didn't know what she wanted. She explained she was in a difficult situation but really liked Jackie and wanted to—"Okay,"

Jackie said, cutting her off. "Call me when you know what you want."

According to Jackie, she cried for a week. Then the phone rang. "Hello," she said, answering on the first ring.

"Oh," my mom started, "I, um, this is Terry, and, uh, I've, um, decided I'm ready to, uh, date you." My mom still laughs when she recounts the conversation. "I was thinking that I was just going to leave a message."

Jackie is always quick to add, "And I was thinking, *I'm going to be with this person the rest of my life.*"

About a year later, and exactly three months before my moms' commitment ceremony on September 21, 1996, President Bill Clinton signed into law the Defense of Marriage Act (DOMA). DOMA, a bill sponsored by then–Speaker of the House Newt Gingrich—who was carrying on an extramarital affair—and signed by President Clinton—who was later impeached for lying about an affair of his own—explicitly defined marriage, in the federal government's eyes, as between one man and one woman, ostensibly to protect the sanctity of the institution. More damaging, however, was the language that granted states the right to refuse to acknowledge a marriage between a same-sex couple married in another state.

When a straight couple is married in Iowa, their marriage is recognized in all fifty states because the federal government requires them to do so. Married straight couples don't lose any of their rights when they go to visit family in Florida—or any other state, for that matter. A pair of opposite-gender first cousins from Iowa could go down to Alabama and get married, where marriage between first cousins is legal. The Iowa government is then required to recognize that couple's union, even though they would not qualify for marriage in our state. But if my moms go down to Alabama, even though they fulfill the marriage requirements and are married in Iowa, they are no longer recognized as such by Alabama's government. Because of DOMA, my moms are, at the time of this writing, legal strangers in forty-one states.

My moms' marriage is also not recognized by their employer, the Department of Veterans Affairs, which provides the federal government's health care service for our men and women in uniform. Worse, my moms have to check the "single" box on their 1040 forms when filing their federal taxes. The legal reality is that *all* same-sex couples, married or otherwise, are "single" as far as the federal government and nearly all state governments are concerned. This allows employers and other businesses to deny same-sex couples spousal rights, such as health and dental insurance benefits. It enables a person's family to deny that person's significant other the right to attend his or her funeral. It also enables a person's family to prevent that significant other from maintaining child custody rights after that person's death.

DOMA declares in its heading that it was designed to "define and protect the institution of marriage." Yet the definition it gives states that the word *marriage* "means only a legal union between one man and one woman as husband and wife."

So let's be clear. Marriage, as far as the government is concerned, has nothing to do with commitment or love or responsibility or honesty. It is not romantic, and it is not reverent. It is only a legal union and a civil contract. Period.

This is a far cry from what I've learned about marriage as

I've watched my moms live and love together for the last sixteen years.

A wedding is a tremendously intimate act expressed in a profoundly public fashion. As much as the ceremony means to the happy couple, it also serves another purpose: to show friends and family, to show the world, "Hey, we're two people who are in love. We are promising our lives to each other and we want you to know it. Now it's your job to hold us to our word."

Even though my moms' ceremony provided nothing legal whatsoever—none of the 1,138 benefits the federal government grants based on marital status, no visitation rights at the hospital, no survivor social security benefits, no surviving partner benefits, and no custody guarantee for Jackie—the part that mattered most, their shared, public commitment to each other, was authentic.

They were married, yet that entitled them to exactly nothing at all. Except that Jackie, who my mom insisted stay in the guest bedroom until they had shared a public ceremony, finally got to move into my mom's room.

For months after my moms' commitment ceremony, Jackie's mother refused to speak with her. It would be just over two years before we all showed up for Christmas at Jackie's parents' house as one big happy (and loud) family. Jackie's mother, Esther, whom we had never met, opened the front door, and before we even stepped into her house, I asked, "Do you think Jackie should be married to a man, not my mom?"

Unfazed by the diminutive seven-year-old standing in front of her, without hesitation, she replied, "Yes." Jackie flashed her a look, and Grandma Esther quickly added, "What? You don't want me to lie, do you?"

It was an illuminating moment. No, Jackie did not want her mother to lie, and Esther knew it. Honesty was a value she had instilled in Jackie decades earlier, and honesty was the foundation upon which my moms built their relationship and rooted our family.

Trustworthiness became an important aspect of my own life and a big part of Scouting. All the merit badges and rank advancements revolve around a Scout meeting the necessary requirements and being honest about what he's done. Scouts have to be honest and realistic with themselves about what they do to satisfy the requirements. After all, what's the merit of a title without the skills to back it up?

Whether I was training for sports or advancing the ranks on my ascent to Eagle, my moms were always honest with me about what I had to do in order to be successful—this has been a powerful blessing and a saving grace. They taught me that success is a choice. You don't always win, and I'm glad my moms never subscribed to the everybody's-a-winner parenting style, because that's not how life works. If you want success, whether it's monetary, sports related, or simply your right to marry the person you love, you have to be honest with yourself about the challenges you will face and the work that will be required to achieve your goals. Without this clarity, without this honesty, we are lost.

Each night, my family and I would sit down with our plates covered in food, and my mom or Jackie would ask us about

our day. After explaining the (incredibly interesting) goings-
on of our lives, Zebby or I would usually broach the month's
value from the book *Teaching Your Children Values* pretty
quickly, so we could get it out of the way and focus on eating.
In retrospect, I'm glad my moms made these conversations
such a focus, but at the time they were just another obstacle
between my food and my stomach.

As I grew older, I started asking what had brought the
two of them together. "Her teeth," Jackie joked, taking a bite
of a chicken leg. And with a smile, Terry would look back
across the table at Jackie and say, "I can't see myself with
anyone else." Beneath the modest jesting, though, I see now
that it was their shared values and their mutual appreciation
for the content of each other's character that united them.

I remember sitting around the table as my moms helped
me grasp the difference between something that was true and
something that wasn't. A few years later, when Zebby was
ready for it, they'd repeated the lesson. Terry asked a series of
questions. The task was to discern which statements were
true. "The sky is green," she'd say.

"Not true," I'd reply.

"Ants are bigger than elephants."

"Not true," I'd say.

"We see with our eyes."

"True," I'd say. In each instance, the answer was rather
beside the point. It was an exercise designed to help us understand the nature of truth and falsehood.

Each chapter in our values book ended with an exercise to
accentuate that lesson. At the end of our month on honesty,
as suggested, we made "the Honesty Pact," which was our

promise to one another that our words and deeds could always be trusted. Honesty wasn't just something we talked about around the dinner table—I watched them live their truths every day, and they helped me define my own.

A friend of mine once observed that how we remember the past—each event's specific memory—is indicative of how it affects us today. If we aren't honest about those memories, if we aren't honest with ourselves about our own histories, what hope do we have for successfully navigating the present, let alone the future?

Looking back, I think my moms' determination to instill in me the drive to pursue truth is one of the reasons I seek out as much information as is reasonable before making an important decision. It's why I draw on scientific—not anecdotal—evidence in justifying my support of same-sex marriage. Until multiple peer-reviewed studies can clearly demonstrate and explain the harm homosexuality has on both individual people and society at large, I will continue to support the recognition of same-sex unions and the advancement of LGBT rights. Were such contrary studies to surface, I would seriously reconsider my position—Scout's honor.

THE MERITS OF TRUTH

Gays and lesbians often have to hide a truth that our society has decided is singularly defining in order to be seen as more than just a "homah-*sek*-shu-al." In this way, society attempts to describe, with one simplistic label, a group of people it cannot understand— does not *want* to understand—discarding this truth as some easy-to-make "choice." As though we all wake up one morning, crack our knuckles, and decide today is the day to pick a sexuality. And, in refusing to learn more, society fails to appreciate that my moms are good people with strong values who work in the field of medicine first. They are lesbians second.

I like to think that the same is true for me, too. (That I'm a good person. Not a lesbian.) If I had to list my identities by order of importance: I'm a good man with strong values first, and the son of two gay moms around seventh or eighth, if that. There are many more aspects of my identity that are much more important to me—being an Eagle Scout, a Unitarian Universalist, an entrepreneur, an American. Being, as the Scout law dictates, someone who "keeps [my] promises" and makes honesty "part of [my] code of conduct." This isn't to say that I don't love my moms, but that their sexuality, or even that they're both "Mom," just isn't that important. Who they are has manifested itself in all those other aspects of my identity, and that, in my mind, is what's most important.

But society—and even some of my family—disagrees. Truths, after all, are only rarely universal, and in an increasingly polarized world, even the universal ones—such as the Golden Rule to treat others the way you want to be treated—are called into question.

At our family's first Christmas dinner, it became difficult for our relatives to look past one truth and see the rest, not so unlike how people are sometimes unable to look across lines of skin color or faith, blinded by the one obvious truth contrary to their own. This was something Terry dealt with for years after coming out to her family. Christmases and Thanksgivings with her religious parents and one of her far-right, Evangelical Christian brothers, were occasionally awkward and stressful. But as time passed, the importance of that truth diminished as everyone realized that she was still the Terry they had always loved before she came out—nothing had really changed.

This realization was not so immediate for Jackie's side of the family. Though her brother and his wife and kids came around pretty quickly, Jackie's parents didn't budge. Grandma Esther, who was in her sixties, had been a committed Catholic her whole life. Eugene, Jackie's father, was suffering from Parkinson's disease, a degenerative disorder of the central nervous system, and losing his health rapidly. His abilities to move and think were greatly impaired by his advancing condition.

At the time, I was not capable of understanding why Esther struggled so greatly with Jackie's sexuality. Now I see that she wasn't just struggling with Jackie, she was struggling with everything. As Grandpa Eugene's health declined—the man she had been married to for nearly forty years—she was leaning more and more on her faith for support. And clarity is not something the Catholic Church lacks when it comes to sexuality. To even challenge, let alone refute, that clarity would be to call into question the infallibility of the very pillar upon which Grandma Esther was leaning for support.

But hiding from the truth of one's sexuality does not make it go away. Running from the truth leaves it chasing you. I discovered how that feels at a young age and realize now that it only makes an uncomfortable reality even worse.

The first time I remember smudging the truth about my family was in fourth grade, when a cute little pigtailed girl at my new elementary school asked, "What do your mom and dad do?"

I was the new kid, the awkward, pudgy transplant from Wisconsin to Iowa City, with the heel lift in his left shoe and the two moms at home. Joining a cadre of kids who had already been together for four years is grade school torture. My eyeballs surveyed the crowd of unfamiliar faces playing on the rubber-padded playground.

In Marshfield, when I had been asked that exact same question, I hadn't been hesitant to respond that I didn't have a dad and both of my moms were doctors. (Which wasn't really a lie so much as I didn't understand the difference between a nurse and a physician.) None of my peers in preschool through third grade had ever given me trouble about having two moms, so I had no reason to bend the truth.

That changed when we moved to Iowa. After our move, I had participated in an Iowa City summer camp program for local youth. We were just old enough that when one of my fellow camp members found out I had two moms, he mocked and bullied me relentlessly. And now, as I found my footing at my new elementary school, I knew that being different was dangerous.

"My mom's a doctor," I said, answering the girl proudly. Then, as confidently as possible, I added, "And my dad's a lawyer."

"Cool," the little girl said, skipping off to play with the friends she'd known since kindergarten, unaware that she had just rocked my world.

I stood there, feeling like a fourth-grade nothing, and tried to convince myself that I wasn't a liar. I knew that lying was wrong, and for all I knew, my father really was a lawyer—1033 had been studying to become one—and she hadn't asked about my other mom.

Years later in high school, the biggest guy on our football team asked me in the locker room before practice, "So what are your parents' names?" I was caught off guard, and my mind went blank.

"Excuse me?" I asked, feigning momentary deafness. "Sorry. I didn't hear you."

"What are your parents' names?" he repeated.

It was then that I realized my parents had gender-neutral names. Their names alone did not betray the truth of their sexual orientation in any way. "Oh," I said, looking up at him. "Jackie and Terry." I shut my locker, grabbed my helmet, and jogged out to the field.

Honesty for the win.

CHAPTER 4

Kind

I'm often asked what the biggest difference is between grow-ing up with two moms and growing up with a mom and a dad. It's a funny question to me because people pose the ques-tion like I've got a control group to compare it to, like there was a time in my life when I had one mom and one dad. As far as I can tell, there aren't a whole lot of "side effects" from growing up with two moms. But there's no denying that there are at least a few. Specifically, having two moms made me an easy target in school among classmates who, more often than not, wanted their friends to be just like them. We are a society that finds comfort in what we know, and there is comfort in what is like us.

The go-to insult among boys in school is to question an-other boy's masculinity. I always think of the scene in *The Sandlot* when Ham delivers what is the supreme, baddest, ul-timate insult: "You play ball like a *girl*!" (If you haven't watched the movie, go put it in your Netflix queue. This can wait.) I think part of the reason boys think calling another boy a girl is insulting is that, from a young boy's perspective, a girl is very foreign and strange, and initially that's kind of scary. But obviously that wasn't the case for me. I knew that, while there were some physical differences, they were primarily aesthetic.

My moms taught me you aren't supposed to treat girls any differently from boys, just like you aren't supposed to treat white kids any differently from black kids. That's what equality means. But, I suppose, someone has to teach you that. Now, are there differences between a girl's life experience and a boy's life experience? Yes. Are there differences between a white kid's life experience and a black kid's life experience? Yes. But those differences do not mean they should be *treated* differently. The Golden Rule applies to *all* others, not *some* others.

Regardless of whether or not a person is different from us, we should treat him or her how we want to be treated, unless we have tremendous cause to the contrary. And I have a hard time believing that race, gender, or sexual orientation—three traits over which there is no control—qualify as "tremendous cause." Actions, after all, are infinitely more important than identity.

My fourth-grade classmates obviously disagreed.

When we moved to Iowa City, I was already the new-comer, an outsider, but add to that the whispers that I was "the kid with two moms," and I had a target on my back.

One morning early in the year, a kid named Travis, one of those boys who always had something to prove, made a crack to the effect that I "didn't have a penis."

"So what?" I said. To be honest, I wasn't sure what his point was. It wasn't true, but even if it was, why should it matter? My moms had raised me to believe that while boys and girls were kind of different, it didn't really matter which one you were. Neither one is better or worse than the other. So my response to this barb was indicative of at least one difference of growing up with two moms: I didn't feel like it was a big deal whether I had a penis or not. I wasn't offended by having my gender called into question because, in my mind, everyone was equal, and someone's gender didn't make him or her better or worse.

Travis, however, leaped on my so-what response and immediately began telling people, "Zach doesn't have a dick." I wouldn't have even cared, really, if the other kids hadn't found it so funny and been so mean about it. His sidekick, Brad, quickly coined a new name, which would immediately ignite years of torment. I became known as "No-Balls Wahls," a moniker I wouldn't escape until junior high, when I shot up almost a foot and gained nearly fifty pounds.

Funny how that works.

But on that day of my christening, there was no such escape. I walked in the door of our new ranch-style house, hung my coat in our living room closet, and felt the weight of "No-Balls Wahls" draped around my neck. Worse, these kids were now broadcasting, in the meanest inflection possible, that "No-Balls Wahls has *two* moms."

For a couple of weeks I tried to cope with the insults without telling my parents, afraid that they'd be hurt if they found out that their sexuality was causing me pain. When I began disengaging from class, my teachers noticed and mentioned to my moms that something was clearly wrong. After some persistent questions on Terry's part, I finally opened up about what was going on. I wasn't very specific, but I explained what they were calling me and that they weren't being nice about it. I didn't mention that they were teasing me about her sexuality specifically, but her instincts knew they were. When she asked me if they were saying anything about her being a gay woman, I just looked away.

My moms gathered our family around the dinner table to discuss the situation. Terry's first concern was not to punish those who were doing the bullying or even to stop them. She first wanted to make sure I knew how to stand up for myself without resorting to violence.

In college Terry had earned a black belt and become an award-winning women's tae-kwon-do free fighter, routinely dominating tournaments across the Midwest. She still likes to recall the story of the time she was driving some folks to their martial arts studio, a dojo, and for the whole drive there one man couldn't stop talking about how much he hated gay people and how if he ever met a homosexual he would beat him or her to a bloody pulp. Once they arrived at the dojo, Terry got out of the car and mentioned to the fellow that, well, she was a homosexual and she'd be more than happy to spar with him if he wanted. The blood drained from his face, and he collapsed into a series of rapid apologies, insisting that, no, he hadn't meant it, he was just frustrated and he definitely didn't want to spar with the five-foot-eleven black-belt woman four ranks ahead of him. Oh no, not at all.

He didn't say much on the drive back home.

Back around the dinner table, Terry introduced me to a technique called "fogging." This method resonated with her self-defense background because it essentially worked by confusing the antagonist and using his own rhetorical weight against him. Think of it as linguistic jujitsu.

"When somebody starts saying mean things to you," she began, "think of ways you can get around what they're saying." I wasn't entirely sure what she meant. "You can't let them keep the focus on you. You need a phrase you can use to distract them."

My first choice was "My mom's a black belt and she could kick your dad's butt." We decided against that one. Despite her black-belt background, Terry kept violence—verbal or otherwise—as a last resort.

"How about 'I feel sorry for you'?" I offered.

"But why are you sorry for them?" she asked.

I didn't really know. I wasn't, really. I was sorry for me and just wanted them to stop.

Then, she asked, "Maybe because they're trying so hard to get attention?" And with that phrase, something clicked.

"Yeah. Yeah," I said. "Hey! 'I feel sorry for you, because you're trying so hard to get attention.'" I nodded my head vigorously, emboldened by the idea of a new defense mechanism. "Yeah."

"That's great!" my mom said. "Now, let's practice."

My moms then took turns pretending to say mean things about me, and each time I rebuffed them with our new phrase: "I feel sorry for you, because you're trying so hard to get attention." By the end of dinner they were positively beaming.

First-grader Zebby, who had been listening silently, blurted out, "I want to *frog*, too!" To this day, it's still one of our favorite Zebby-isms.

The next day when my moms got home from work, I still had a silly grin on my face. They were eager to hear about how my day had gone. I recounted how on our way back from the gym that morning, Joey, the kid who had recently been bullying me the most, started mocking me, talking about how awful having no balls must be, and I was probably so bad at dodgeball because I didn't have a father to teach me how to throw. Shaking, but remembering our practice from the night before, I kind of mumbled, "I feel sorry for you," but then trailed off.

"What?" he asked, looking down at me and sensing blood in the water.

Turning around and drawing myself up, I said, "I said, 'I feel sorry for you. I bet it feels bad needing all this attention so bad.' "

There was dead silence. You could hear the moment.

After one of the tensest standoffs in my life, the kids on my dodgeball team—and a few on his—suddenly burst out laughing. It was the first time I can ever remember anybody else taking my side in such an exchange.

My moms smiled with enormous pride, and Terry pulled me in for a bear hug—a mama grizzly, if you will.

Not everyone thinks having two moms is something to be used against you. My family was actually blessed by the kindness of many folks over the years, much of it from people you might not expect to be so benevolent toward a family like mine. Boy Scouts is a classic example.

When I joined Cub Scouts—Boy Scouts for younger boys—as a kindergartner, my primary goals included journeying out into the wilderness, racing Pinewood Derby cars, and learning how to use a pocketknife. I wasn't even aware that my participation would be, for some, controversial.

It was a lot less controversial than you might think, though. Maybe part of that had to do with the Midwestern habit of not asking too many questions about things that don't concern you, but I think most of the non-controversy stems from the fact that my moms were eager participants in the organization and were there in the flesh. It's much easier to be nasty when you're not dealing with someone face-to-face. (I think this is one of the reasons cyberbullying is increasingly prevalent in our society.) When somebody is an anonymous figure, foreign and distant from your own position, it's infinitely easier to pass laws and policies discriminating against that person. Yet when my moms—two gay women barred from engaging in Boy Scouts at a national level—got involved at the local, face-to-face level, the members of our Cub Scout pack could see that they were regular people with the same worries, concerns, hopes, and dreams as everyone else. They were welcomed with open arms.

I know that many people think of the Boy Scouts of America as a homophobic organization. After several lawsuits, they have removed from their official website their formal policy that stated "we do not allow for the registration of avowed homosexuals as members or as leaders of the BSA," but the culture of intolerance still permeates much of the group's leadership, both at local and national levels. Yet, when I came home from the orientation night at Washington

Elementary and announced I wanted to join Cub Scouts, my moms were both very supportive and never once second-guessed my request.

And this juxtaposition—that my two gay moms fostered in me a passion shared with equal enthusiasm by an organization so traditionally conservative as the Boy Scouts of America—really gets to the heart of the equality issue: the degree to which a parents' sexuality actually affects a child's character.

There are values I learned in Boy Scouts that might be thought of as feminine by some—kindness is a perfect example. There are values I learned from my moms that are probably thought of as more masculine—values like courage, discipline, and responsibility. The thing I find interesting about being the son of two lesbians is that I don't feel either masculinity or femininity is better or worse. They taught me that these values are all equally important regardless of the gender of the child. Courage in young women is as equally important as kindness in young men.

There were certainly times, though, especially in those early years at my new elementary school, when I felt anything other than well-rounded and healthy. There were definitely days when I wished I had a dad, but such wishes were always fleeting, and never did I wish a dad would replace one of my moms. I'm sure that this will be taken out of context, but whenever I wished for a dad, it wasn't because I actually wanted or needed a dad, it was just so I could fit in. Sometimes in awkward situations I'd lie and tell people that my dad occasionally took me skiing, not because I was ashamed of my parents or had this fantasy where he'd swoop in and save the day, but because, given the situation, a lie was simply less complicated than the truth. This wasn't a rejection of my parents at all. My dishonesty simply flowed from my desire to not be teased or bullied because of how my family was composed.

I'm not gay, but I know how it feels to be in the closet.

There is a perpetual struggle that we all go through to fit in, fueled by the recognition that being different can be used against you. And it hurts. As the last kid to arrive at the fourth-grade party, and the kid with two moms to boot, I was the last kid picked for teams in sports and the first to be the punching-boy piñata if there was ever the need for one.

If we hadn't moved from Wisconsin, I would have still had my tight-knit group of friends. I occasionally imagined that if I were still in Marshfield, my gang would have been romping around the neighborhood, causing trouble like we used to. The girls there loved me. (I guess I treated them better than most other boys did.) I had routinely gotten in trouble for kissing them during recess. (Another advantage of lesbian moms: I knew girls didn't have cooties.) And the boys and I had happily bonded over our love of *Star Wars* movies and LEGOs. It had been good.

Back in Marshfield, when kids found out that I had two moms, it was like, "Oh, okay, let's go play." The fact that I had two moms mattered as much as what they did for a living, which is to say, not at all. We were able to quickly move on to the things that *actually* mattered, like how much fun we could have in one another's company. Since they were willing to learn more about who I was—that I liked *Star Wars*, magic tricks, and LEGOs—the fact that I had two moms was no big deal. I didn't need to shy away from the truth, because at that age no one cared. We were too young to understand why gender, race, or sexual orientation could possibly matter, too young to be afraid of a difference in any of those traits.

At that age, kindness is the default setting.

About two months into fifth grade, my mom called me to the basement. As we sat at the bottom of the stairs, I was painfully aware that this would be one of those "serious talks." My mind was racing as I tried to figure out what the imminent onslaught was going to be. For the life of me, I couldn't even fathom a guess. "Zach," she began, "I just got off the phone with Cody's dad."

"Cody . . . Haynes?" I asked.

"Yes," she said.

Oh. Maybe this wasn't so bad. I knew Cody. He was a grade younger than me, and we were in Cub Scouts together, though not in the same den. His dad was the Cubmaster, the highest-level leader of the pack. Cody and I weren't exactly best buds—he never came over to hang out—but we certainly weren't enemies.

"Okay," I replied. "And . . . what?"

"Well, Cody's dad told me that you've been . . . rough on him lately." My confusion continued. My mind searched for what his dad could possibly be talking about. "Cody feels that you've been kind of *bullying* him."

"That I . . . *what*?" I was completely aghast. Whatever I'd thought she might be about to say, that definitely wasn't it. I was horrified. I knew what it meant to be bullied. How could I *possibly* be doing that? I was a nice kid. I wouldn't hurt . . . Then, it hit me. I knew what Cody was talking about.

The older kids had been doing it for a while. They had started practicing a variation of the Vulcan neck pinch from *Star Trek* on one another. Instead of touching the area between the shoulder and neck, though, they just grabbed the back of the neck, using the thumb, pointer, and middle fingers. It didn't really hurt, but it wasn't exactly painless, either.

I had been doing that to Cody. Without realizing it, I had stopped fogging and started trying to prove to the kids bullying me that I was just like them. And as my mom and I sat at the bottom of our stairs, to my disgust and horror, I suddenly realized I was.

This understanding slowly began to spread across my face, and Terry looked at me with two-pronged concern. Looking back, it's clear that while she was waiting for further confirmation that this bullying had taken place, she was deeply disappointed in both me as a young person and in herself as a parent.

Searching for words and on the brink of tears, I choked out, "I . . . well . . . I think I know what he's talking about, but that's not how I meant it!"

My mom held me as I burst into sobs of protest and self-loathing.

Now, this is my realization: Most bullies don't consider themselves bullies. They don't really think about what they're doing. They just do what they do—bully, tease, and mock others—because it feels good and can sometimes make their own pain go away. They don't realize that they're doing wrong because, to them, it feels right. Exerting power over others mediates the pain of being powerless at home or with friends, somehow soothing a damaged sense of self.

I had been roughed up by my peers and was troubled by my mom's failing health—which no one was discussing—and I was acting out. The values my mothers had instilled in me told me that what I was doing was wrong—and very much so. Once my behavior was brought to my attention, I wanted to make amends and change my ways. That, I think, is the real testament to the parenting of my mothers.

But, much to my mortification, Mom insisted that I call Mr. Haynes and apologize to him over the phone, and then to apologize to Cody in person. I'll never forget dialing that phone, shaking as I entered their phone number out of the school directory. It was a short conversation, my burning desire to end it kept me on point, but it was memorable. Mr. Haynes knew, too, that my behavior had been out of character and suspected it was unintentional. He told me that he appreciated my calling and apologizing. He said he'd relay my message to Cody, but asked that I say something to him personally.

The next day at school I kept trying to find the right time to talk to Cody. I wanted to give him both an apology and an explanation for my behavior—say that I hadn't intended to hurt him. After a couple of failed attempts and false starts, I finally approached him after classes were over, knowing I could not face my mom at dinner not having completed my mission.

I talked really fast. "Cody," I said. "I'm sorry I was picking on you. I didn't mean to hurt you. I hope you can forgive me." He nodded without saying anything and then turned and hurried away. I don't blame him. That's what I would have done if somebody else had said to me what I had just said to him.

Don't attract any more attention. Head down. Quickly move on.

I knew all about that.

THE MERITS OF KINDNESS

Since I was a little boy, my moms have impressed upon me how important it is to be kind. Actually, kindness was one of my favorite values in Scouts ("A Scout knows there is strength in being gentle. He treats others as he wants to be treated.") and was a favorite chapter/month in *Teaching Your Kids Values*, because, in my mind, it was so simple. And, as a bonus, it made me feel good. I remember, after one particularly heavy snowfall, I shoveled my neighbor's driveway for no reasons other than it was a nice thing to do and I had nothing else lined up for the evening. I also found that kindness often comes back around with a payoff. A month or so later when our snow blower broke, that same neighbor kindly plowed our driveway and made my moms (and me, who would have had to get up at five to shovel it) very happy.

I'm aware that not every one is kind.

Though I reject the notion that bullying is a "rite of passage" that everyone goes through—and *should* go through, as some even say—I cannot deny that experiencing and overcoming that bullying taught me that people can't make you feel inferior without your consent, and no one will stand up for you until you stand up for yourself. You will encounter mean, nasty people, you will run into roadblock after roadblock, and life will not always be easy. But with the right state of mind, the right skills (I still use fogging once in a while), and the right values, you can overcome damn near anything you find in your way.

Every day after school in fourth grade, a bunch of my classmates would hang out at the house of a kid named Brian. His yard bordered the school and kids would go there to play boomball (softball using a kickball). Brian's yard was landscaped to be a small diamond with a dugout under their porch. Even though I desperately wanted to be one of the kids invited over, I think I only played there twice.

What I've realized is that being kind is simple, but it's not always easy. Overcoming the scorn your peers might aim at you if you invite the loner to a game of boomball is tough, no matter how good a person you are. But extending an invitation is quite simple. It's a subtle difference, but it's one that greatly helped me understand the nature of kindness and incorporate that value into my everyday life.

When I was a junior in high school, I joined the Speech and Debate team. That first year, a teammate and I worked on a duo interpretation piece called *The Boys Next Door*. In duo interpretation, the two participants perform a published work that they adapt for the duo event. *The Boys Next Door* is a play about a social worker in a group home for men with mental handicaps. The climax of the play occurs as one of those men sheds his disability to address the audience as a cogent, articulate man navigating the struggles of his situation. The dozens of hours I spent reading, crafting, and performing that piece made for a powerful education in the need for being kind to all those we encounter.

But the most powerful lesson from that experience came in a single, almost accidental, moment of kindness.

When I was in sixth grade, there was a student with mental challenges in our class named John McMannis. I couldn't tell you exactly what his challenge was—maybe Down syndrome— and it's really beside the point. He would be in class every day, and a bunch of us would work with him to help him get through assignments, learn how to type, that kind of thing. Even though he was older than all of us, we went on to middle school, and he stayed behind. I didn't see him again until I was a junior in high school.

Heading back to class, I saw John for the first time since we were sixth-grade classmates at Weber. I immediately recognized him as I walked toward him. He was looking in my direction, but he didn't make eye contact—his eyes always looked slightly out of focus—and just because it seemed like the natural thing to do, I smiled and said, "Hi, John."

He looked toward me, but not at me, and said back, clear as day, "Hi, Zach!"

I stopped dead in my tracks—stunned—and watched as he kept walking without a care in the world.

And it was in that moment that I started to fully appreciate the importance of even the smallest of our everyday words and actions. Although it might not seem like other people notice—sometimes it might seem like people are *incapable* of noticing—our words and deeds echo much, much further than we can ever hope to understand.

There is strength in kindness, and that strength is contagious. But coupled with that realization is the understanding that silence, both in word and deed, is permission. Inaction, the refusal to respond, is itself a form of response, one of the most pernicious sorts. In the words of Holocaust survivor Elie Wiesel, "Neutrality helps the oppressor, never the victim."

And though the core of my understanding of what it means to be kind was ingrained in me at an early age, I've continued to learn more about the value, and about myself, as I've grown. I was a freshman in college when I encountered a commencement address delivered by the great American author David Foster Wallace. The address, titled "This Is Water," begins with a short story that has stuck with me and has become one of my favorite allegories. It goes something like this:

> There are two young fish swimming in a stream one day. They swim past an older fish headed in the opposite direction. The older fish says, "Morning, boys," with a nod. "How's the water?" The two young fish nod back and keep swimming upstream. After a little while, one of the young fish turns to the other and asks, "What the hell is water?"

There are many different interpretations of this brief exchange, but I understand Mr. Wallace's point to be that the young fish don't understand their existence is sustained by this thing called water. The older fish knows that there is a unifying force that binds them all together, that unites them. This unifying force, as it pertains to us, is human interaction.

If you look at the word "kindness," its root is "kind," like "humankind." "Kind," as a noun, refers to a group of people or things that share similar characteristics—our humanity. To be "kind" as a verb, is to recognize our shared characteristics, our shared humanity, and to remember to respect one another, because beneath the veneer of our aesthetic differences is the inherent worth and dignity of every living person.

This is water. The water that we're all swimming through is sometimes so obvious we can't even recognize it. It is the fact that, at the end of the day, we're all just people, nothing more and nothing less. We're people with hopes and dreams, flaws and failures, friends, family, secrets, and surprises. Today, when I find myself in a frustrating interaction with another person—a screaming baby in the seat behind me, unapologetically awful service at a restaurant, a moron who cuts me off on the highway—I try to take a deep breath and remind myself that this is water. This interaction is the medium through which our lives are lived, and without it, however painful or frustrating it may be at times, we would be nothing. To treat others any differently from how we want to be treated is to destroy ourselves.

CHAPTER 5

Friendly

Losing old friends is hard. Making new friends is often even harder. But, shortly after fifth grade started, I got lucky. Really lucky. For the school scavenger hunt I was randomly paired with Nic Jewell, that year's "new kid." He had just moved to Iowa from Colorado and had the same birthday as my former best friend in Wisconsin. Maybe we took that as a sign, or maybe it was because he didn't really know anybody and after a year of school I still didn't really know anybody, but either way, we became fast friends.

Though we were in different classes, Nic and I were on the same "team," which meant that our two classes would often get to do activities together. For the school's scavenger hunt, our list of things to find was primarily comprised of bits and pieces of nature. It was the pinecone that stumped us. Although there were pine trees in the backyards of people whose properties bordered our elementary school, we got called out by a teacher when we tried to leave school property to grab one. We didn't win the scavenger hunt, but this time I was fine with losing, because I had found a friend.

Shortly after we met, Nic introduced me to a card game called Magic: The Gathering. We connected over that, and more than a decade later, we still occasionally throw down a game or two on a slow night. It's a fantasy-world game that simulates a battle between two or more dueling wizards. You summon creatures or cast spells from the cards you have in your hand to wipe out your opponent's twenty life points. We'd usually split our games, each winning about half. (Although, he might tell you he wins three out of five.)

We liked all things fantasy, particularly *The Lord of the Rings*. We'd often walk back to his house together after school because his parents worked from home and mine would still be at the hospital. We would lose ourselves in the world of Middle Earth and all of the elves, orcs, dwarves, and wizards that inhabited it, lords of a realm limited only by our imagination.

But three short weeks into our budding friendship, we were all brought crashing back to reality.

Around 7:50 A.M. central time, I returned to the cafeteria of Weber Elementary. The morning's before-school program I was in had just finished playing a game in the gym, and I remember joking with my teammates as we walked through the doors, jumping up to touch the metal frame and, as always, missing.

I remember seeing the TV perched in the corner of the room set to channel seven. The screen showed two skyscrapers, one burning. Those of us just coming back from the gym assumed the obvious—that for some reason, we were watching a movie. I recall seeing one of our counselors crying. Something was wrong. And then it dawned on me: This was live news.

Those of us in Mr. Lawson's class ran to our homeroom. Mr. Lawson was working at his desk when we got there, drinking coffee from an absolutely ridiculous sixty-four-ounce Kum & Go mug. We told him to turn on the TV.

We watched United Airlines Flight 175 hit Two World Trade Center, the South Tower, though, from the camera angle, it looked like the North Tower had experienced a second explosion. I expected it to immediately collapse, but it didn't. The angle then changed and we saw that it was in fact the South Tower—a second plane had crashed into the World Trade Center.

We all shared a feeling of collective disbelief as the meaning of a second crash sunk in, arrested by a quiet combination of shock and fear. This was no accident. Two planes were down, and no one knew how many were still in the sky.

Students were beginning to trickle into the classroom for school when the Pentagon was hit, at which point it became obvious that America was under attack. A classmate of mine asked me if I thought we were safe. Repeating words I had just heard from the CNN anchor, I told him that "they" had just hit the nerve center of our national defense. It was hard to say.

I was scared.

We watched as the towers collapsed. We gasped as the clouds of white dust filled the city, engulfing people on the streets. I was struck by the bravery of those who rushed toward the still burning, twisted wreckage. But I did not cry. My mom had told me that when President John F. Kennedy was shot, her teacher cried. *How many people were in those buildings? On those planes? What was next?* Mr. Lawson was stoic. I suppose we were all shocked beyond tears.

Down the hall, Nic's class was already back to their lessons. His teacher felt it best to concentrate on schoolwork. I'm not sure if I'm glad we watched or not.

By the time the bell rang for lunch, a fourth flight had been downed in a Pennsylvania field by a group of courageous passengers, saving the lives of countless hundreds at the cost of their own.

After American airspace was secured, we filed into the cafeteria. Principal Haverkamp announced over the intercom that we had just experienced a horrific attack against our country and then asked us to observe a moment of silence in memory of those who had lost their lives.

All afternoon we watched cable news replay the images of those 767s slamming into the WTC complex, forever changing the landscape of our minds and searing into our memories the events of Tuesday, September 11, 2001.

That night my family piled onto our couch and watched President Bush address the nation. I remember being inspired by his speech. I felt the swell in my chest of patriotism and pride. I recognized it as the same feeling I got during Cub Scouts meetings, but even more potent and powerful.

The next morning at school, we stood outside the Team Four wing as all five classes joined in reciting the Pledge of Allegiance to our flag, Mrs. Henry guiding us through the words—words I already knew by heart from my time in Scouts.

For a brief moment, on September 12, the labels didn't matter. We were all Americans.

At Cub Scouts that night, we set aside some time to remember the victims of the attacks and to pray for the survivors in critical condition. Our pack held a small memorial service in our school's cafeteria, and I remember lighting a candle in vigil immediately after Nic lit one.

After some rousing words from our Cubmaster about the importance of both strength and perseverance, we broke out into our dens and Jackie led mine through a conversation about what had happened the day before. We were all a little shell-shocked and couldn't fully comprehend what had happened, let alone know what, if anything, would happen next.

I was glad Jackie was leading the conversation. She doesn't talk a lot—I get my speech patterns from my other mom—but when she does, she thinks it through and always offers a useful and unique perspective. She has a penchant for saying exactly what needs to be said and nothing more.

She explained that the people who had flown the planes into the Twin Towers had been radical Muslim extremists, but she wanted us all to realize that they were not representative of all Muslims. She told us that radical extremism is not isolated to any one race, color, class, or religion. The execution of the Oklahoma City bomber, Timothy McVeigh, had taken place only a few months prior, but the monstrous actions of Mr. McVeigh, a white male veteran of the United States military, had not reshaped how we thought about white men. This shouldn't be any different.

And maybe that was part of what was so terrifying about

the Oklahoma City bombing. Although I was too young to remember the actual event with much clarity, I know now that shock and disbelief seized people as they read about a man who looked like a son, a brother, or even a father to most of us, a man who, at face value was an intelligent, religious, U.S. veteran—someone many would have been glad to call a friend. But even as they read of this man's inhumanity, their perception of people like him didn't change. The day after his bombing, we were not struck by suspicion when we saw white guys driving delivery trucks. That's not the nature of suspicion.

We are suspicious of difference.

Nic says that it was at an early campout after he first joined our pack that he found out my two moms were, well, my two moms, that my family was "different." He and his dad were having a private chat away from the fire, and his dad told Nic that Jackie and my mom were together, "like a couple." And he wanted Nic to know that he thought they were nice. It was the only thing his dad needed to say.

Then he told Nic, "But you should probably wait for Zach to bring it up, though. He might not feel comfortable telling you."

Nic respected his dad's request. I only found out about that conversation when I started working on this book. That discovery is a phenomenon I have experienced a number of times while reminiscing about the past in order to write about it now. My life has felt so average that I've had to seriously examine my experiences in order to find even the slightest deviation from what a "normal" family goes through. I always thought my family was pretty typical, except for the fact that my mom had MS, but even on that front, many families struggle with chronic disease. Terry's diagnosis was just another reminder that it can happen to *any* family.

But I never tried to hide anything from Nic. We just hit it off right away. I couldn't tell you why or how, but we clicked. I think when I first introduced Nic to my moms, I said, "This is Jackie and this is my other mom, Terry." It was probably obvious which one was my biological mom, as I was already almost taller than Jackie, but he didn't ask either way. He was my friend, and he knew it didn't really matter.

While Nic's friendship made the time I spent at school infinitely easier, I slowly found a groove in the other aspects of my life, too. I particularly enjoyed the time I spent at Sunday school and found my fellow Unitarian Universalists to be very accepting of my familial situation. Nearly all of them seemed to think my two moms were interesting, but that was it. It was nice to have a space where I knew people weren't asking a lot of questions, whispering behind my back, or gawking whenever my family walked into a room.

I got pretty close with a pair of brothers who were also going to our new church. Jake was a year older than me, and Mike was a year younger. We had similar interests—they also played Magic, were in Scouts, and shared my love of football—but what I most appreciated was how laid-back they were. To them, that I had two moms was no big deal.

Looking back, I wonder if part of why they were so nonchalant about the whole thing is related to the fact that they spent a few months of their childhood growing up in Nigeria, when their dad was stationed there for work. They knew what it was like to live in a culture different from their own and that those different customs and beliefs were no less worthy of their respect. I think that by experiencing such vast and worldly differences at a young age, they have both been blessed with the ability to look past the superficial as they go out into the world and meet new people with different backgrounds and ideas.

This is certainly true of their father, Cliff, as well. In fact, it was Cliff who showed me how to use a razor. One night I was over at their place hanging out with Mike, and Cliff noticed the peach fuzz on my lip and asked me if I'd like to know how to use a razor. I said sure, and about five minutes and a few cuts later, I knew how to shave.

When I got home from Mike's place, as clean-shaven as an eighth-grader could be, Jackie noticed that my fuzz was gone. Terry, who's not particularly good at noticing that kind of thing, didn't notice at all.

"Oh, cool," Jackie said.

"Yeah," I told her. "I'm pretty psyched about it."

And that was about it.

Our parents don't know everything, and sometimes we have to count on the friendship of others to learn more. My moms' close friend Sylvester helped get me interested in investing at a young age, something my mom knows a bit about, but there was no doubt that Sylvester was much more of an authority on the subject. My mentor from church, who worked at a brokerage firm in town, would build on Sylvester's early coaching and helped me create a solid foundation of fiscal responsibility. Looking back, I think it's pretty clear that from whom you learn how to shave, throw a baseball, drive a stick shift, balance your checkbook, or mow the lawn isn't the important thing. What's important is knowing how to do those things and having access to people who can teach you if you want to learn something new. That's what friends are for.

The point is that not all people have the same beliefs and customs, and similarly, not all people have the same skill sets. My moms might not have been able to show me how to shave my face, but they sure weren't able to teach my sister how to use makeup, either. And guess what?

We both turned out just fine.

THE MERITS OF FRIENDSHIP

On a Scouts trip once, Jackie had to explain that the word "queer," in some contexts, is used as a homophobic slur for a gay person. I had no idea.

My friends and I were playing Smear the Queer, which was this game where you would get the football and run around and tackle one another. After playing for a while, I went back to the campsite to get something to drink. Jackie and another mom, who had stepped in for her husband who was on a business trip, were starting to get hot dogs ready to throw on the fire.

"What are you guys doing?" Jackie asked.

"Oh," I said, "we're just playing Smear the Queer." Jackie shot me a look, like I'd said something really, really wrong.

"You're *what*?"

"What?" I asked. "Why arc you giving me that look?"

"Don't you know what that means?"

"What, 'smear'? Yeah, it's like to tackle."

"No . . ." she said, hesitating, as though she didn't believe me. "*Queer.*"

"Doesn't it mean different or strange?" I asked.

"Zach," she said, "it's a euphemism for gay."

I didn't know. Really. I wasn't sure how to respond. I just stood there frozen. Finally, I asked, "Oh, okay, what do I do? Do I apologize?" The guys I was playing with were my best friends, and they didn't mean anything by it, certainly nothing on a personal level. She just looked at me, so I said, "I'm sorry." The other mom then launched into a rant about how her daughter had been saying all these things about other girls, calling them sluts and lesbians. She had found a diary . . .

I had to walk away. It was too uncomfortable. I went back to the guys and said that we should call the game Crush the Carrier instead of Smear the Queer, and everyone was like, "Oh, okay, sure. Let's call it that."

And even though a game called Crush the Carrier might not sound too friendly, how we arrived at that name and, more important, why, is in my mind a classic example of what friendship is all about. Friends teach you things, stand by you, and support you, even—and especially—when it isn't easy.

Friendship is a bond. It's a connection that two or more people develop and nurture, a relationship that can be called on when needed and from which all benefit. Friendliness, on the other hand, is a state of mind. At its core, friendliness is a simultaneous recognition of the differences that exist among us and a conscious decision to look through those differences to see the similarities that unite us. As Scouts taught me, "A Scout is a friend to all. . . . He seeks to understand others. He respects those with ideas and customs other than his own."

Once, on a ski trail in Minnesota, I nearly skied straight into a sign that read, "Respect: you've got to give it to get it." I think friendliness is a lot like that. You have to be friendly to others before you can expect others to be friendly to you.

I've also learned that before you can be a good friend to others, you have to be a good friend to yourself. This requires a certain level of independence, self-esteem, and a positive, steadfast outlook on life. Before you can inspire confidence in others, you have to be confident in yourself. Before you can support others, you yourself have to stand on a firm foundation.

The Boy Scout Handbook says, "Friendship is a mirror. When you have a smile on your face as you greet someone, you will probably receive a smile in return. . . . Accept who you are, too, and celebrate the fact that you don't have to be just like everyone else. Real friends will respect the ideas, interests, and talents that make you special."

This is incredibly important, because we don't see the world as it is. We see the world as we are. What we see is a reflection of ourselves, of our biases and fears, our ideologies and beliefs. If we are ourselves friendly, we see friends everywhere, and if we aren't, we see enemies lurking behind every corner. If we keep our guards always up, we miss opportunities to deepen our understanding of the world, because there is always something to learn from others.

Newt Gingrich once observed, "People like me are what stand between us and Auschwitz. I see evil all around me every day."

I'm not sure who Newt is hanging out with—or if that's just a natural by-product of living in Washington, D.C.—and maybe this is just because I'm from Iowa, but I don't detect a whole lot of malice when I'm out and about. I wouldn't say that I'm the most friendly, happy-go-lucky guy in the world, but I still see a lot more good than bad around me. I think most people are trying to get through their lives, enjoy their careers, love fully, and raise their kids to be happy, healthy people—and hopefully having some good desserts along the way.

As the early-morning events of September 11 unfolded, our commitment to the American promise of life, liberty, and the pursuit of happiness was openly challenged. On September 12, we woke up and things were different. We were all Americans. But "we" didn't apply to everyone. Even as we flew our flags and rallied together in renewed patriotism—that moment of unity seared into my generation's collective psyche—distrust flowed all too easily. Muslim and Middle Eastern–born American men and women, who were and are just as American as the rest of us, now stood cloaked in the shadow of omnipresent suspicion.

It's important to ask ourselves why.

After all, the day after the Oklahoma City bombing, most Americans didn't wake up with a fear of the white guy next door. There was no second-guessing U.S. veterans and no fire-bombing of Catholic churches. Timothy McVeigh didn't look different, but there's no denying that beneath his all-American veneer, he was vastly more different from the American mean than the Muslim family living down the street.

I wonder if foreign-born taxi drivers in New York City felt a twinge of fear as white guys got in their cabs after that day of infamy in Oklahoma.

In our rush to give people their labels and put them in their respective boxes defined by their looks, customs, or beliefs, we forget that such simple classifications do not help us understand the world. The uncomfortable reality is that people do not fit into neat, prepackaged stereotypes. I might be the "kid with two moms" to you, but I am not like all kids with two moms, and not all kids with two moms are like me.

Being friendly means you don't just put people in their box—you try to find out who they are. And this goes for everybody, no matter what box someone might try to put you in.

Supporters of same-sex marriage and other LGBT rights cannot blindly ascribe the label of "bigot," "hateful," or "ignorant redneck," to all those who oppose their agenda. Although there are certainly some people opposed to same-sex marriage who are all those things and more (I'm looking at you, Fred Phelps), one does not necessarily qualify the other. To assert otherwise is shortsighted and arrogant and presumes that you have nothing to learn from the experiences of anyone else.

If you don't take the time to talk with people and get to know them—if you aren't friendly—it's easy to go through life thinking that we are all vastly different from each other in profound, deeply meaningful ways. How can we hope to understand the world if we aren't willing to understand each other? How can we hope to understand each other if we aren't willing to engage each other? And how can we hope to engage each other if, when we see somebody who seems to be even slightly different from us, we look away?

If you do take the time to stop and ask questions, to learn more about people of different faiths, nationalities, and races, you'll learn that there is far more that binds us, more that unites us, than separates us.

We forget that sometimes.

CHAPTER 6

Reverent

It was fairly late one night when my moms got back from their latest visit to Ohio, and they were upset, definitely not themselves. Terry's limp was more noticeable, distinctly worse after a long day of travel, her face somber. Grave, almost.

Their trips to Ohio had become a regular occurrence, though their purpose remained unclear to Zebby and me. I joked with Nic that they were probably corporate spies, because, let's be honest, it's genius. Who would expect forty-year-old lesbian spies? I hadn't questioned them much about their travels, perhaps because when Mom and Jackie would disappear for the weekend our babysitter would be "in charge." That meant staying up late, playing computer games, and eating all kinds of awesome contraband.

I helped them unpack their bags and start the laundry, and we all sat down at the dinner table for a late supper that our sitter had prepared for us before she left. We exchanged some welcome-home pleasantries, and after running through that evening's example of the value of self-discipline, Terry glanced at Jackie, that grim look still on her face, and nodded.

Jackie reached down into her backpack, which she carries instead of a purse, and pulled out a handful of professional-looking tri-fold brochures. After a brief moment of choked silence, Jackie led us through a difficult conversation that fundamentally changed the trajectory of our family. Jackie told us that right before our move to Iowa in 2000, Mom had been diagnosed with multiple sclerosis. Jackie went on to tell us a few things about the disease and how they were treating it. Her words sounded foreign. I sort of stopped listening. Terry really didn't have anything to say, not because she didn't have something to contribute, but because she couldn't find the words to do so.

I would later learn that in Ohio they'd been visiting the Cleveland Clinic, one of the world's most advanced MS treatment centers, looking desperately for ways to slow Terry's physical deterioration. Depending on the expert, her prognosis was either "really bad" or "really, really bad." And her diagnosis had just been adjusted from relapsing-remitting MS to secondary progressive MS—the pace of her decline was accelerating.

After the conversation was over and I had bussed the family's dishes, I quietly retreated to my bedroom, overcome by shock and uncertainty. I tried to read some *Star Wars* books to take my mind off what we had just discussed, but that didn't work. So I just lay on my bed, thoughts wandering, simultaneously wishing that I had paid closer attention to Jackie's lecture and incredibly glad that I hadn't.

When everyone else went to sleep that night, my worried curiosity got the best of me, and I slunk back out to the kitchen to carefully review the brochures. There was a list of symptoms that, even though I was a good reader, was way above the average adult's understanding, let alone that of a smarty-pants twelve-year-old.

"Optic neuritis," *I have a book of optical Illusions . . .* "Nystagmus". . . "Ocular dysmetria." *What?* "Cognitive dysfunction." *Oh, wait. Cognitive. We had that in vocabulary. That means to think. Dysfunction. Is that like malfunction? I know what those are. Spaceships in* Star Wars *have malfunctions all the time. Is her thinking broken?*

I kept reading and slowly gathered that MS was a disease that affected the brain and spinal cord, resulting in the loss of muscle control, vision, balance, and sensation. The bit about losing feeling didn't make much sense, as I knew that my mom had been having painfully strong sensations in her face.

The "zingers," as she'd come to call them, were intense bouts of face pain that she first felt in medical school. She describes a zinger as an electrical sensation that is much like putting your finger in an electrical outlet, a debilitating burn that will not cease on any terms but its own. Sometimes they'd get so bad that they'd push her up against a wall. While powerful medication can, for a short time, put her zingers on the defensive, once they start, not even formidable narcotics like morphine can stop them.

One of the brochures folded out to show a medical diagram of a female body. It had a list of symptoms—from blurred vision to muscle weakness—and arrows pointing from the list of words to almost every part of the body. There was also a dramatic statement that I understood with frightening clarity: "There is no known cure for multiple sclerosis."

In Scouts, I swore every Monday night "to do my duty to God," a responsibility I took seriously and which has served to light the way through dark times. Faith became particularly crucial as we navigated the trials and tribulations of Terry's multiple sclerosis, a journey made even more difficult by our knowledge at the outset that it could only be treated—it would never go away.

Until her diagnosis, my faith had largely been a learning experience. I spent my weekly Religious Education class at our Unitarian Universalist church learning about myself, the Bible, the nature of other faiths, and the history of my own. Now church became more than just a learning experience and a place to make new, nonjudgmental friends. My faith was now something upon which I leaned for support.

If not for the struggles we had with MS, I don't know if I would understand why my Grandma Esther is so reluctant to question the Catholic Church's position on gay marriage and homosexuality. I see now that to even consider challenging the Church's position would be to question the strength of her own foundation. And even though I can usually understand why she is so rooted in her beliefs, it's not always easy for me to remember this. I was extraordinarily disappointed when she refused to come down to Iowa in 2009 for my moms' official marriage, and I have at times expressed that frustration in inappropriate ways.

Terry's mother, Grandma Lois, also had issues with the whole marriage thing. When Terry and Jackie had their commitment ceremony, she told them she wasn't coming even though my moms picked her birthday as the date for the service. She said she had to work. My mom knew her own mother. It wasn't about work. It was about her religious beliefs and the generational discomfort with the very idea of who her daughter is. All things considered, my mom took it in stride. Her dad was dead, and her mom wasn't coming, so she invited her mom and dad's longtime best friends, Sylvester and Darlene. Sylvester and Darlene were not just friends of the family; they proved to be the kind of friends who helped my family remember to be a family. En route to my mom's commitment ceremony, Sylvester and Darlene decided to stop by Grandma Lois's house, where Grandma Lois was hard at not working, to remind her of a thing or two.

For people still grappling with this issue, the battle is not between political parties or religious beliefs. It's not a question of constitutionality or even of morality really. The struggle is not between you and someone else, but between your head and your heart. Religious beliefs—whether they are in the divinity of Christ, Allah, the Buddha, or whom-/whatever else—should never be an excuse to treat people badly. At the end of the day, respect for others' beliefs comes down to the kind of person you are or aren't.

Sylvester and Darlene, two people to whom their Catholic faith was the world, showed Lois how to get out of her head and to live with her heart, to recognize what she knew fundamentally to be true: The "straight" love she had felt for her husband was no different from the "gay" love Terry felt for Jackie. Love, our hearts know, is love, and it is a beautiful thing.

"Terry's like our daughter," Sylvester told Lois. "We're going to be there for her and you need to be there, too. You don't miss your daughter's wedding."

Grandma Lois relented.

Sylvester, Darlene, and Grandma Lois pulled up in their pickup truck at the church right as we got there. Sylvester was beaming, his toothy grin on full display. "We weren't going to miss this day!" he yelled out of his rolled-down window in his gravelly Midwestern voice, well-accustomed to making himself heard over the roar of massive farm equipment. After he parked his pickup, a visibly flustered Grandma Lois gave us all big hugs.

Sylvester and Darlene's kind hearts showed my Grandma how to be happy—sincerely happy—for her daughter and for us. They also set a striking example for me of what Christianity and reverence are all about. Before Sylvester died in the summer of 2011, both he and Darlene were active in their church as religious education teachers. To me, they embody the best of all religions: thinking of others before themselves.

One November afternoon in sixth grade, I had just finished my final rounds for Safety Patrol (pretty much a glorified hall monitor) and was setting out for home. It was a Friday, and I had plans to hang out with Nic before going to see a vaudeville variety show my sister was in, followed by pizza and watching the *Lord of the Rings* trilogy for the gazillionth time. Mrs. Nelson, the Safety Patrol coordinator, caught me as I was leaving the school grounds and asked me to follow her back to the office. Even though she assured me that I wasn't in trouble, I had a queasy feeling in my stomach. The first thing any kid being told to follow an adult to the office presumes is *uh-oh*.

We walked into the principal's office, and Terry was sitting in one of the chairs, her face red and wet with tears— something that was not yet a common sight.

My mom looked at me, her lips curling downward and trembling. Unable to find her voice, the task fell to Mrs. Nelson, who began, "Zach, it's your Grandma Lois. . . ."

Grandma had been staying with us for the last few weeks. Terry's decision to bring her family back to her home state of Iowa had cut the travel time between Grandma Lois's house and ours from four hours down to two. Since she was now widowed and had never fully recovered from a heart attack seven years prior, she came to stay with us quite a bit. We had even begun referring to the large guest bedroom in the basement as "Grandma's room."

I loved when Grandma Lois came to visit, because it almost always meant she'd be making one of her legendary pies. Lemon meringue, banana cream, and chocolate were the most popular, but when blueberries were in season, she also made exceptional blueberry pies.

But now the chocolate pie Grandma had baked earlier that week was to be the last one she'd ever make.

"Your Grandma Lois," Mrs. Nelson repeated as I sat in her office, my orange Safety Patrol sash draping over the side of my chair. "She died this morning."

My mind flashed back to the night before when Terry and Jackie were at the dress rehearsal for Zebby's show. Grandma Lois had stayed home to spend time with me—she'd see the show on opening night—but instead of working on a jigsaw puzzle like we usually did, I'd chosen to use the time to play computer games. It hadn't seemed like a big deal.

I didn't cry at the news of her death. I felt numb, arrested by the realization that the brewing skepticism I had felt about God since Terry's diagnosis had now been transformed into full-fledged doubt. When you're young, and probably even when you're not, the loss of someone you love clarifies the fragility of your connections to the rest of those around you and makes you question everything.

When my mom and I got home from school that afternoon, Jackie wrapped me up in a tight hug, and it was only then, as the initial shock began to wear off, that the tears started to flow. Zebby had found out that morning that Grandma had died and had subsequently stayed home from school with Jackie. But Zebby had made up her mind that the show had to go on, a decision she knew Grandma Lois would have supported and encouraged. After embracing Jackie, I hugged Zebby, pulling her close, the squabbles of our sibling rivalry momentarily forgotten.

The four of us stood in the kitchen of a family now missing a member and prayed. Silence settled.

After a few moments of stillness, Terry said it was probably time for Zeb and her to head to the show. Nodding, Zebby went to the refrigerator to grab some food for the road. With a quiet, jagged groan, she removed from the shelf Grandma Lois's last piece of chocolate pie.

I couldn't focus on the play. Jumping dogs and juggling couldn't grab my attention. I was still fixated on how I'd spent the night before, upstairs playing computer games while Grandma Lois read one of her romance novels down in her room. Alone.

I couldn't help wondering why God would take Grandma without letting me say good-bye.

Backstage, Zebby was having her own troubles with the task at hand. She had worked so hard on her performance and steeled herself to do it, but moments before she was set to take the stage and sing her piece, a kid simply said, "I heard your grandma died." It was too much. Zebby broke down and couldn't go on.

When she didn't enter at her cue, I knew immediately what had happened. I felt bad for her. I felt bad for my mom. I felt bad for me.

After the show, as my mom dealt with the aftermath of Zebby's backstage breakdown, Jackie drove me home. She turned her yellow Nissan Xterra into the driveway, and we climbed out and just sort of stood in the front yard. There was not yet snow on the ground, and the winter air was settling, the sky was clear.

"You know," Jackie said, "the other nurses told me to tell you that the first star you see tonight is Grandma looking down on you." I looked away, shivering. "But you're old enough, I think, to know that this is just going to be hard. But, it'll get better, I promise."

Nodding, I hugged her and we went inside.

The funeral was in Elkader, Iowa, a small farming community in the northeastern part of the state, where Grandpa John had been laid to rest. Grandma Lois was buried between her husband and her daughter, Mary Ellen, who had died twelve hours after birth. After a church service and a brief graveside service in the bitter cold, we drove in Jackie's Xterra to the family farm, just north of town, where John and Lois had raised my mother and her two brothers.

During the twenty-minute drive, not a word was spoken.

We got out of the car, and Zebby carried the small translucent Tupperware container down to the creek. I followed behind with a small spade. Zebby found a spot she liked not too far from the icy stream, and I dug into the chilled, muddy ground.

Carefully, Zebby removed the last piece of Grandma Lois's chocolate pie and gently set it into the shallow grave. We took another moment, as Jackie hugged Terry, who was struggling to stay standing. With a heavy sigh, I lifted the shovel and buried the pie—knowing I would never get back that last night I didn't spend with Grandma Lois.

THE MERITS OF REVERENCE

I think the big point of reverence is that we all have our beliefs, we all have our systems of support and faith and reverence, and that's great. They are important. We should respect one another's systems and beliefs. We should *not* try to change other peoples' systems against their wills, and we should not inflict our systems on others if such infliction results in the harm of another human being.

Personally, I don't really care what your religious views are as long as you aren't inflicting needless pain on others simply because their beliefs are not congruent to your own. This is a common viewpoint among UUs, because most of us believe that nobody has a monopoly on truth. (There's an old UU joke about how the best way to terrorize one of us is to burn a question mark into a UU's lawn.) And while this is certainly a UU belief, it is a Scouting belief as well. Muslims and Hindus and Buddhists and Catholics and Protestants all come together in the fraternity of Scouting, which encourages us not to question one another's motives or beliefs but to celebrate them and to learn about one another. *"A Scout is reverent toward God. He is faithful in his religious duties. He respects the beliefs of others."*

Yet, as in all democracies, there will be differences. I look at the Declaration of Independence and read, "All men are created equal." Rick Santorum looks at the Declaration of Independence and reads, "All men are endowed by their Creator." I believe that rights are innate and inherent in the nature of being human. Rick Santorum believes that rights come from God and that without God, there would be no rights. I simply disagree.

And while my faith is a central part of my life, and I certainly know that it is incredibly important to many, many people, there is no doubt in my mind that a dozen hands engaged in hard, charitable work will change more lives than thousands of hands clasped in prayer.

I would watch as my mother literally willed herself out of a wheelchair, staying up late night after late night, working relentlessly to beat the disease that had robbed her of the future she had dreamed of sharing with our family. I see the miracle in her recovery and believe that our family has been blessed beyond what any of us deserve, but I cannot see the hand of God in Terry's revival.

Just as we do not see God regenerate the missing limbs of the quadriplegic veterans my moms care for in their professional lives, I am unable to believe that God takes a direct hand in the health of any one person or people. Yet God is a source of strength and guidance in difficult times, and without God, I do not know how our family would have fared during the worst of Terry's MS.

When I tell people that I'm a Unitarian, I almost always get a blank look. It is not a particularly widespread denomination and only rarely ever mentioned in pop culture. (Regular viewers of *The Office* might remember that Phyllis's husband, Bob Vance, is a UU and that at one point Angela thought his religion was the reason that the office was cursed.) I explain that it's rooted in some of the more tolerant branches of Protestantism and draws many of its beliefs from deism—a highly popular religious philosophy in the Enlightenment Era, which counted Benjamin Franklin, President James Madison, and Thomas Paine among its members. Unitarian Universalism, the religion of presidents John Adams, John Quincy Adams, and Thomas Jefferson, shares with deism an appreciation for natural law, a respect for reason and epistemology, the belief in one God, and skepticism of the supernatural.

There are seven core principles around which the Unitarian Universalist faith is based, and they are usually presented as such:

> We, *the member congregations of the Unitarian Universalist Association, covenant to affirm and promote:*
>
> *The inherent worth and dignity of every person;*
>
> *Justice, equity, and compassion in human relations;*
>
> *Acceptance of one another and encouragement to spiritual growth in our congregations;*
>
> *A free and responsible search for truth and meaning;*
>
> *The right of conscience and the use of the democratic process within our congregations and in society at large;*
>
> *The goal of world community with peace, liberty, and justice for all;*

*Respect for the interdependent web of all
existence of which we are a part.*

As a young Unitarian Universalist in my Religious Education classes, I learned about and visited sites of worship for
many different faiths around the city, touring a local Muslim
mosque, a Jewish synagogue, many different Christian
churches ranging from the simple Mennonites to the rock-
and-roll Evangelicals, a traditional Chinese ancestral shrine,
and even a Zen studio.

And almost every place we went, if we ran into other kids
our age, we'd encounter the same question: "Wait, you're a
what?"

With a lighthearted sigh, I rolled my eyes and I explained
that I was a Unitarian Universalist. I pulled out the small
chalice-shaped silver pendant hanging around my neck to use
as a prop in my explanation.

The two circles represent duality, the circle of life and the
unity of all things—hence "Unitarian." The chalice is burning, providing us with light and guidance along the way. "The
way to what?" they'd usually ask. Through life, I suppose.
Toward salvation, maybe. That's what the "Universalist,"
part means. Universal salvation.

Not exactly fire-and-brimstone stuff. Both of my moms
turned to Unitarian Universalism after being rejected by the
Christian denominations in which each of them had been
raised. Unitarian Universalism feels that a person's sexual
orientation—something my moms knew they had no control
over—could not be itself a sin and should not confer them to
a second-class existence.

I look at this situation and see an interesting dichotomy. The Bible, after all, is explicitly clear that wives are supposed to be completely subservient to their husbands. Yet our society decided that part isn't right, and that belief has long since left the mainstream of religious and philosophical thought. Even Michele Bachmann, an unapologetically conservative Christian woman, watered down that belief during one of the 2012 GOP presidential debates.

But then these same folks who set aside this belief turn around and say, "Well, yeah, *of course* women deserve the same respect as men, but gay people? No way." I hear this once in a while when I'm out on the lecture circuit and fairly frequently when I'm talking with folks in the rural parts of Iowa.

I usually respond with an analogy I picked up in one of my UU religious education classes. I'm no expert, but in my mind, the Bible isn't a buffet. You can't walk through, picking out only the parts you like and really heaping those onto your plate, while leaving the parts you don't like alone. You especially can't then point to what's on your plate—and only what's on your plate—in an attempt to pass laws.

If you're going to cite the Bible as your justification for marriage being between only one man and one woman and make that definition law, by that line of reasoning, you also need to support laws that would put women to death if they can't prove their virginity at the time of marriage and decree that marriages are to be arranged instead of based on love and that interfaith marriages ought to be illegal.

But nobody argues that. Indeed, the "sin of homosexuality" seems to be, in the minds of some folks, all defining in a way that other sins aren't. Interestingly, many other sins, like adultery, can be overlooked and the people who commit them still welcomed into the flock (Hey, Newt!), but gay people are turned away for their "alternative lifestyle choice," as though, at the first, that nobody else "chooses" to sin, and at the second, that gay people spend all of their time exclusively doing gay things.

I cannot bring myself to think of my moms' sexualities—or anyone else's sexuality for that matter—as the most important part of who they are. My own sexuality simply isn't a large enough part of my life for me to believe it could, on its own, ever accurately summarize me as a person or fully convey the events of my life thus far. Labels like gay or straight, white or black, Muslim or Christian, may make our lives easier on a day-to-day, trying-to-make-sense-of-this-crazy-world basis, but they are a poor foundation upon which to make major policy decisions. More fundamentally, we have to remember that while it is certainly easier to sort people out in our minds along such lines, until you take the time to actually get to know a person, you can never truly know him or her.

There is no label that can ever replace a face-to-face, earnest conversation.

CHAPTER 7

Helpful

My mom knew that the days of riding her bike with the rest of the family were gone but became driven, nearly to the point of insanity, by her refusal to fall further into the confines of her wheelchair. By my junior year of high school, my mom was trying all kinds of different things to abate her multiple sclerosis, staying up all night in the living room poring through medical journals and study after study. Her dreams were not of recovery, but of a slower descent. She was seeing a new physical therapist and had made some pretty significant changes to her diet. But as the year wore on, it didn't seem like she was improving at all.

One afternoon while I was at speech and debate practice, I got a call from her cell. "Hey, Zach," she said. I could barely make out her voice. Her speech was strained, and she sounded exhausted. "Could you come pick me up? I'm at the physical therapist in Coralville."

I cut practice short. When I got to the therapist's office, I found her in the waiting room looking beat. She put nearly all her weight on my shoulder, and we hobbled back out to my truck. She didn't speak on the way home, her eyes were closed and her face red. My truck was old, and I knew that every bump we hit was causing her more pain.

I made dinner when we got back to the house. Terry had stopped eating anything containing wheat, dairy, or eggs (all of which, she had theorized, worsened her condition) and was now eating fruits, vegetables, and organ meats almost exclusively. This severely cut down our family's dietary options, but it made making supper pretty easy. I had mastered the art of preparing my mom's new favorite dish, kale salad with citrus fruit.

As she sat in her special chair at the table, she was silently recharging. I didn't know at the time that she had just finished her first round of electrical stimulation, or "e-stim" for short, which is a form of physical therapy she had first read about as part of her research duties at the VA hospital. Traditionally, elite-level athletes used e-stim to aid recovery after really intense workouts. Using it as a form of treatment for patients with neurodegenerative diseases was unprecedented. Although she was exhausted and unable to speak, she had just completed the first trial of a therapy that would play a large role in a recovery that can only be described as miraculous—and I don't use that word lightly.

But even when it became clear that she was no longer regressing, and was perhaps even making progress, we were all hesitant to get our hopes up. After all, as a doctor, Terry had been the first one to acknowledge that recovery was pretty much out of the question. A rapid turnaround, to go from failing to recovering, seemed impossible.

Then again, she's always had a habit of doing things that everyone else thought couldn't be done.

As her healing progressed, she was able to transition from a wheelchair to an electric scooter. But while her back strength was slowly returning, her stamina was still pretty poor. Despite this, when she heard that I had made it to Nationals for Speech and Debate, she insisted on accompanying our team to the tournament. Honestly, I was embarrassed about it. Even though she could use a scooter at that point, instead of her tilt-recline wheelchair, she was still far from healthy.

The national tournament was a four-day competition, and she would need her scooter to get around the entire time. We made it to the school where the competition would be held in Las Vegas, where the temperature was in the triple digits— hot and dry.

I opened the trunk and reached in to pull the scooter out, but I couldn't get it out. Frustrated, I pulled harder. The scooter was caught on something in the rental van. Under the beating sun, decidedly anxious about the day's competition, and already sweating in my black suit, my patience gave way.

"God, Mom!" I shouted through the van toward her in the front seat. I stopped trying to lift the scooter and let it crash down into the back of the van. I stormed around to where my mom sat, the front passenger door halfway open. "I can't," I told her in a raised, angry voice. "I can't do this right now! You've got to handle it!"

She was just sitting there in a tank top and shorts, white

crew socks creeping up her still-atrophied legs. A look of shock and apology spread across her face, her mouth hanging agape.

In a moment I flashed through all the hardships I'd experienced in my life because of her: dealing with her MS, my fear of people finding out about my family being different, and the silent, torment-induced anger. My mom, even though she could walk for only short distances, wanted to be there to share a triumphant moment with me. She certainly didn't want to embarrass me or complicate things, but she would have never forgiven herself if she hadn't come. That's just who she is. She was trying to be helpful, a mom who went to Nationals to see her child achieve a dream. And, humoring her, I had feigned excitement about her joining us on the trip. But now, I had let slip the truth.

We made eye contact. She was on the verge of tears. Startled by the distress in her eyes, I recoiled, unable to believe the words that had just come out of my mouth. Shame coursed through my body, and I apologized profusely, my frustration with her immediately transformed into self-loathing. I couldn't believe what I had just done. I wrapped my mom in my arms and said, "I'm sorry. I'm sorry. I'm sorry."

Being helpful sometimes means putting someone else's needs before your own. And when you don't meet the challenge—as I failed to do with my mom on that hot, summer day in Las Vegas—your failure sticks with you. You can have the best values, be the most principled person, but we all slip up. Nobody is perfect. It's how you feel in the face of that failure and what you do in response that is indicative of who you are as a person.

My moms have taught by example. Both of their lives have been dedicated to helping others. Each of their careers is in service to those in need, and today they both care for our country's men and women in uniform, working for the Veterans Affairs Hospital and Clinic in Iowa City. Terry, an internal medicine physician, works in the VA's polytrauma clinic, attending to vets who have suffered severe head, neck, or back injuries. These injuries are all major drivers of post-traumatic stress disorder, a mental condition that has been described as a silent killer among those coming home from multiple tours in Iraq or Afghanistan. Jackie is a nurse practitioner working in the outpatient clinic, where she oversees the recovery and rehabilitation of vets, helping them to get back on their feet. They both talk about their jobs with pride in what they do, admiration for those they serve, and a sense of appreciation for having the chance to do jobs they both love.

There should be no doubt that the road to Eagle Scout is a journey of service—to family, to others, and to self. I've always found service to be a humbling and enriching experience. Even today I vividly recall the first time my Cub Scouts pack went to Saint Carol's, an old folks' home in Marshfield, on Christmas Eve. Looking back, especially now, it's nice to remember how eager and anxious I was—we all were—about the whole affair and how happy those folks were to have us there. The visit made for a really nice Christmas.

It was a lesson in how we each possess so much power that we can choose to exert for the benefit of others. Sometimes these choices are so obvious that we don't even realize we're doing something special. I've learned that these opportunities to help improve the lives of others are often staring us in the face.

My weekly Scouts meetings were, for more than a decade, a central part of my family's life. The planning of den meetings fell to the den leader. It was a lot of work—like a teacher planning a lesson or a preacher preparing a sermon—and a den leader could either make or break both the fun and the learning. Like teachers and preachers, den leaders need to be extraordinarily giving people. If a den has a leader who makes each meeting interesting, keeping the attention of all the boys, the den will succeed. Finding dedicated leaders for each level of the organization often proves the most difficult challenge for the Scouts.

For much of my first year in the Scouts, our meetings were little more than poorly organized chaos. With more than twenty first-grade boys on his hands, our den leader had a difficult time making us behave, let alone keeping us on task. Further, he had no clue how to inspire or instruct young minds. After the flag ceremony and recitation of the Cub Scouts promise, our meetings would slide downhill—fast.

At a meeting of all the families, it was decided that the den was too big, and we needed to break up into two groups. That meant we needed another den leader. Knowing what troubles the current leader was going through each week, no one was jumping at the "opportunity." Eyes scanned the room. Who would take on the task? Who would step up and serve?

One hand lifted. It was the hand of the woman sitting next to me.

All the other boys in my den had just gained another

mother. Over the next three years, as the den mother for dozens of Scouts, Jackie exemplified the Cub Scouts motto of "Do your best," and eventually the Boy Scouts slogan: "Do a good turn daily."

Jackie became one of the most beloved den mothers in our pack's recent history, and Terry went on to help out as an interim Cubmaster during the search for a new leader, enabling both of them to know all the other moms and dads involved with our pack. The more the other parents learned about my moms and the values they lived by, the more those values became the defining features of my moms' identities in the eyes of the other parents. Their sexuality, which might be all important in the eyes of the national BSA organization, mattered little to the folks in our pack.

After Jackie raised her hand in Marshfield, she spent hundreds of hours over the ensuing decade volunteering her time to help the boys of my Cub Scouts pack, and then my Boy Scouts troop, learn and grow into mature young men. When we moved to Iowa from Marshfield, our Cub Scouts pack gave Jackie a print of a wolf named Akela—a Scouting symbol derived from Native American traditions that prized wisdom, authority, and leadership. The inscription on the print read, "To the best Akela a Cub Scout could have." They had been as sad to see her go as I had been to leave. Jackie had been so helpful that one of the boys' moms called ahead to a Cub Scouts mom she knew in Iowa City to tell her that Jackie would be a great den mother. The transition was seamless, and the parents and boys in Iowa grew to like her almost as much and almost as quickly as the pack in Wisconsin.

My first Scout memory with Jackie as my den mother is of making dream catchers. Jackie told my fellow Cubs and me that the Native Americans had used dream catchers for centuries to keep bad dreams away while allowing good dreams to pass through. That's something she knew I needed. I had been having night terrors, vividly painful dreams of breaking my femur at daycare when I was three years old, which had left me imprisoned inside a waist-high body cast for three months—an eternity for such a little kid.

There was one recurring dream in particular that was really scary, and I'd been having it for nearly four years. In the dream I was being hunted by a velociraptor. Not just any velociraptor, though, this bad boy had laser guns for eyes—the worst possible combination of my two favorite things. I was still in my body cast, which left me hobbled and incapable of running. The velociraptor would stalk me and corner me. I could hear its breath but couldn't catch my own. Then I'd feel heat as it moved in for the kill. I would start screaming and crying, but I wouldn't wake up. This would wake my baby sister, who would then start crying, too.

I didn't consider whether Jackie was thinking of me when she designed the activity. All I knew was if a dream catcher could stop bad dreams, I was going to make the best dream catcher ever. With the goal of catching those dreams, I remember pondering the selection of colored yarns and beads as if it were the most important decision I'd ever made. This was serious stuff.

We each held a metal hoop in front of us and looked at it as Jackie explained that Native Americans honor the hoop as a symbol of strength and unity. "Unity means we're all together," she said. "Like our den. Our pack." We began weaving a web of yarn at the center of our hoops. The web would entangle our bad dreams, catching them and holding them until they burned up with the first light of a new day. To attract good dreams we wove sparkly beads onto the yarn. These would guide the good dreams through the web. The hole at the center of the web would let those dreams pass through, and they'd slide down the feathers that hung at the bottom and into the person sleeping below. I attached my two feathers and couldn't wait to get home.

Once I hung my dream catcher over my bed that night, I never had a night terror again. Call it folklore, the power of suggestion, or whatever you'd like—it worked. Today dream catchers are a little overcommercialized, but that dream catcher is still hanging over my bed at home. With Jackie's help, I put my night terrors to rest.

One of the biggest events each year in Cub Scouts is the Pinewood Derby, a race of homemade wooden cars built from a BSA-certified kit containing a block of pinewood, plastic wheels, and metal axles. Finished cars are raced on Derby Day down a long wooden track, using the same gravity-powered concept as a full-size Soap Box Derby car. The Pinewood Derby, which was created by a Cubmaster whose son was too young to participate in the Soap Box Derby races, is typically an opportunity for a dad and son to spend some time together carving, painting, and fine-tuning the car with weights to achieve maximum speed. It is well-known in Scout circles that the dads actually do most of the heavy lifting.

But I didn't have a dad, and my moms didn't even have

any tools to speak of, except for the requisite household hammer, screwdriver, and wrench. Stereotypically, you might think that Cub Scouts–leading lesbians like my moms would have an array of power tools, but we had to turn to Jackie's brother Pete in Wausau, who had a virtual Craftsman paradise in his basement—a precursor to the hardware store he would later open. Pete's teenage son, Ryan, had always loved both cars and crafts and agreed to help me with the project. Jackie and I drove up to their house with my four-dollar kit on my lap and a design idea already in my head. I loved Batman, and I was going to race the Batmobile.

Ryan and I worked well together. He was the nephew who had inspired Jackie to get me my first LEGO set, and each year Ryan and I would get new sets on Christmas morning and have them built by Christmas night. My moms would then carefully pack the creations in our car and transport them back to Marshfield like priceless works of art. But carving from wood was a whole 'nother ball game from piecing together plastic bricks.

Ryan and I started with my block of wood and began whittling it down with a band saw and a knife. And by "we," like most of the other Cub Scouts my age, I mean the guy who knew what he was doing. I just sort of sat there and watched while Ryan began bringing the sleek lines of the Batmobile to life.

When I got back to Marshfield with my newly carved car, I painted it a glossy jet-black, added decals, and Tall Mom and I used clay to sculpt a Batman head and torso with tiny pointed ears to put in the driver's seat.

Batman rolled down the wooden track on Derby Day and

lost the race in spectacular fashion. I came in dead last in almost every heat. Disappointed though I was about the loss—I
enjoy winning just as much as the next guy—my pack
awarded the Batmobile Best Paint and Design, which to me
was (almost) better than winning the race.

It was an important lesson. I knew that if I'd tried to
make the Batmobile on my own, I wouldn't have won any
awards and may very well have lost a thumb. But with Ryan's
help, I'd walked away with a top prize.

There's a destructive myth we have here in America about
the self-made man, the hero who rises to the top entirely of his
own volition. While every single person is undeniably capable
of incredible feats on his or her own, it is only with the help
of others—your cousin, your Scout leaders, your parents,
your community—that the greatest accomplishments are
achieved.

THE MERITS OF HELPFULNESS

My mom's descent into the chair was swift and merci-
less, and without help—both in her home and at her
workplace—she would have been left stranded. As
her mobility and stamina declined, the VA modified
her position so she could continue to work. At home
we all picked up more and more chores—helpfulness
was no longer a choice; it was a necessity. My mom
fell from being a fully functional, former world-class

athlete to being incapable of sitting upright in a regular chair. So weak was her lower back that when we would drive up to central Wisconsin to visit Jackie's family for Thanksgiving or Christmas, I would have to use a small harness to strap Terry to the passenger seat in our van. Going to movie theaters together required that she either use her wheelchair or that I bring along one of her zero-grav chairs that reduced the stress on her back by suspending her on a hammock-like, bungee-cord seat.

To be honest, I found this ritual of strapping her to her chair in public far more embarrassing and uncomfortable than the fact that I had two moms accompanying me. It felt awkward to find myself in the role of caregiver at such a young age and highlighted the helplessness of the woman who cared for me. But when you're helping others, sometimes you just have to get over your own discomfort. That is, after all, what it means to put someone else's needs before your own.

And this relationship went both ways. Even as Terry worked late, night after night, in an effort to find some treatment, some intervention that just might help, she always made sure that she was staying in touch with Zebby and me. She'd work with Jackie to go over our homework assignments, our essays, and our planners. When she saw that I was slacking on my Algebra 2 problem sets, she found a tutor (much to my chagrin) to help me get back on track. In regards to my personal life, she always maintained an open-door policy, and if I ever felt like I had something to talk about with either her or Jackie, they were both always willing to put whatever they were doing on hold to listen to my problem of the day.

My moms were both textbook examples of what it means to help other people at all times, one of the promises each Scout makes when he repeats the Scout oath. The Scout motto asks you to be prepared and the Scout slogan reminds you to do a good turn daily. These three commitments work together: you promise to help, you are able to help because you have learned how and are prepared to do so, and you decide to follow through and actually help because you care about other people—whether they're your mom, a fellow Scout, the little old lady struggling with her groceries, or the guy who happens to lose his cell phone while watching fireworks on the Fourth of July.

Scouts want the best for everyone, and act to make that happen without a hope for monetary gain or other reward. I once read that if you brag about doing the good turn, it doesn't count. It's not a formal rule or anything, but I appreciate the sentiment. I've always thought of character as what we do and who we are when no one else is looking.

At its core, the Boy Scouts of America is a service organization. Being helpful isn't just a tenet of the

Scout law, it's the underpinning of every Scout's mission and, for a lot of us, service was why we kept showing up week after week and year after year. After all, *"A Scout is concerned about other people. He does things willingly for others without pay or reward."*

Every fall my Boy Scouts troop would distribute empty plastic bags on peoples' doorknobs for a national BSA program called Scouting for Food. We'd then return a week later to collect the bags, each hopefully filled with donations of food for those in need. We would then sort the bags and distribute the food to various charitable food pantries. It always made me feel good when Jackie drove my patrol around to collect the donations, knowing that hungry people were going to get fed—not just in my community, but all across the country as Scouts collected tens of millions of pounds of food. I found purpose in being a part of something larger than myself.

The highest rank in Scouting is Eagle, and achieving the highly coveted position requires a few difficult steps. You must serve as a leader in your troop for at least six months while at the level of Life Scout, earn twenty-one merit badges, and demonstrate that you live by the Scout oath and Scout law in daily life using personal references.

Further, every Eagle Scout candidate is required to do an Eagle Scout project, a rigorous community service endeavor. The project must be to the benefit of a local nonprofit organization other than the BSA, a requirement that highlights the community service–oriented nature of the Boy Scouts. To serve your community without payment is to learn a lesson about putting others first. A Scout project often benefits the whole community and requires a big investment of time and energy on the part of the Scout. It is a hands-on lesson in both leadership and management. You gain the vision and motivation necessary to do the right thing and the skills and confidence to do things right.

The thing I really liked about the Scouting for Food program, besides its benefit to the hungry, was the fact that the Boy Scouts would get the community involved in doing good, facilitating community engagement. As important as our participation and organization and work were, without the generosity of the community, the program would not work. That felt right to me and gave me tangible proof that people want to give back. I decided to think of other ways I could use that model, and since I've always loved books, I figured a natural pairing of the two would be a "Scouting for Books" project.

We wouldn't be able to cover all of Iowa City, so I picked a handful of well-defined neighborhoods. I made a series of phone calls to stores to ask them to donate supplies. I got Zephyr, a local print shop, to print copies of an announcement so that I could tell people what was going on, and Hy-Vee, a local grocery chain, to donate plastic bags. I then got friends and people in the troop to help distribute bags and collect books in a method similar to Scouting for Food.

Jackie and Terry provided much-needed moral support and guidance but left the actual planning and execution to me. At this point Terry couldn't stand without the aid of two canes. She would spend most of the day reclined in her wheel-chair, as she didn't have the lower back strength to sit upright. But she still wanted to help. While Jackie shepherded me around in her Xterra on collection day, making numerous trips and carrying lots of books, Terry waited back at the collection site in her zero-grav chair.

The First United Methodist Church, where our troop met on Monday nights, had given me permission to use their basement as a staging ground and storage site. We collected more than five thousand books, and once they were all stacked and sorted, the basement actually looked like a library—or my dream home.

Then came distribution based on book genre. The Veterans Affairs Patients Library got the war books, the romance books, and anything that seemed it might be of interest to an "older audience." The children's books were split between the University of Iowa's hospital and clinics patient libraries and the Iowa Department of Education's Learn to Read program, which sends books home with disadvantaged kids.

Without the help of my friends, family, fellow Scouts, and community members, I would never have been able to collect five thousand books and put them in the hands of the patients, veterans, and young kids who deserved them. In many ways, my Eagle project brought full circle the lesson that began in Ryan's basement with only an idea and a small block of wood: When we share a vision and face our hopes and challenges together, we are capable of so much more than when we face them alone.

CHAPTER 8

Courteous

On top of the personal battle with MS that we all struggled with at home, we were unwittingly caught in the crossfire of a political war as well. On September 2, 2004, as I sat with my moms in the master bedroom watching the Republican National Convention, I realized that some people thought my family had no place in America's future, that our family wasn't a real family—we were just a "lifestyle choice."

I don't like thinking about the LGBT rights debate in terms of words like "battle" or "war." Such terminology makes me uncomfortable because it inevitably posits another group of people as "the enemy." But as I watched the other side present its political platform, it suddenly became clear to my eighth-grade mind that the people speaking believed my family shouldn't exist and the fact that we did exist was a threat to "family values." If it was up to them, my family wouldn't just be considered "different," we would be against the law.

I wasn't really sure what to think. My school assignment had been to watch the Republican Convention's speakers and write down my thoughts on what they said, so I had been camped out with my moms in front of their TV for nearly three hours. On my lap lay a yellow legal pad covered in notes I had furiously scribbled while trying to keep pace with the evening's speakers, recording the most egregious, incendiary proclamations of the mainstream Republican Party.

The assignment wound up being an eye-opening exercise.

Watching the suits—all well-groomed, official looking, and presidential seeming—get up and talk about the dangers of terrorism one minute and the threat of gay marriage in the next was nothing new for either of my moms, but it was terrifying to me. I remember thinking how glad I was that Zebby was already asleep. She was definitely too young to hear that her family and other families like ours were being singled out by our government, specifically targeted by a major party's platform.

I was young and confused, not about my family and the values we had, which were still crystal clear, but mystified as to why these people would say things that were, in my mind, obviously not true. Most frustrating of all was that these people—nice-looking, ostensibly well-intentioned folks—would stand up and, in one breath, say things with which I fully agreed but then, in the next, suggest that the commonsense American ideals they had just defined stood in direct opposition to families like mine. I knew that no such conflict existed.

Looking back, I realize that they would have *liked* for us to be Godless, hedonistic, freedom-hating deviants trying to force our "lifestyle" on others. Quite simply, they didn't *want* us to share their values—they wanted a monopoly on virtue. They wanted us to be different, and vastly so, because if we were fundamentally different and not just "separate but equal," they could justify taking our rights away. But if we weren't so different, if we had more in common than we did in contrast, then they could not. There aren't many aspects of this debate that are simple, but even an eighth-grader could understand this part.

In my notebook, I wrote down quotes from some of the lauded speakers. The quotes I recorded each started out with a statement I found reasonable, before taking a decidedly different and alienating tone:

> *"We step forward by expressing tolerance and respect for all God's children, regardless of their differences and choices. At the same time, because every child deserves a mother and a father, we step forward by recognizing that marriage is between a man and a woman."*
> —*Governor Mitt Romney*

> *"Marriage is important not because it is a convenient invention or the latest reality show. Marriage is important because it is the cornerstone of civilization and the foundation of the family. Marriage between a man and a woman isn't something Republicans invented, but it is something Republicans will defend."*
> —*Senator Elizabeth Dole*

> *"In this world of change, some things do not change: the values we try to live by, the institutions that give*

our lives meaning and purpose. Our society rests on a foundation of responsibility and character and family commitment. [. . .] Because the union of a man and woman deserves an honored place in our society, I support the protection of marriage against activist judges."

—*President George W. Bush*

I looked down at my notebook and then up at my moms, sitting side by side against the headboard of their bed. I was confused. My moms were married. I had watched them walk down the aisle and given them their rings. When I asked my moms why the people on the TV were saying that marriage was only between a man and a woman, they explained the legal standing of their own union—it had none. In the eyes of the law, despite everything I knew about them and about our family, they were not *really* married.

When I go back and look at these quotes and think about the arguments that these folks were making on national television, they weren't being rude, per se, or even using pejoratives to describe families like mine. At face value, they were being polite, and that's important. Even at the state hearing in Iowa where I spoke in January 2011, despite some people literally calling for gay people to be put to death, the tone of the evening was mostly cordial. It is a subtle difference, but I would argue that these speakers were being polite, not courteous.

When you're being courteous, your actions are formed out of respect for the person you're interacting with. It's a state of mind. As *The Boy Scout Handbook* reminds us, "Being courteous shows that you are aware of the feelings of others." But that's not what the people who make this argument are doing. They're only thinking of themselves.

After all, no one is asking them to get gay-married or even requesting they buy a wedding gift for those who do. This isn't about trying to "convert" anyone. If you're opposed to gay marriage, don't get one, but do the courteous thing and don't prevent others from doing so. In the words of Thomas Jefferson, "It does me no injury for my neighbor to say there are twenty gods or no god. It neither picks my pocket nor breaks my leg."

But that's not how most opponents of gay marriage approach this issue. They think that homosexuality is a special kind of sin and that gay people are a special kind of citizen— citizens who do not have the right to marry those they love. At that January public hearing in Iowa, I watched as one of the speakers asked a Republican state representative how his same-sex marriage to his husband had any negative effect on the representative or the representative's marriage. How, the speaker wanted to know, did his marriage threaten anyone? The politician just laughed and said, "Don't be ridiculous. You're not *actually* married." And that was all. The smirk on his face said the rest.

The refusal to recognize how someone identifies himself is to imply that you are a better judge of who that person is than he is of himself. To suggest that anyone or any family that is not a mirror image of you or your family somehow lacks validity is the height of disrespect and discourtesy.

What I've realized is that despite what we may see on TV or read about in magazines—the endless system of binaries that has been forced on us by a media culture that promotes homogeny but thrives on division—a family is not a straight, legally married WASP couple with two and a half kids, a dog, and a white picket fence. A family is a group of people who love one another. As I observed in my testimony, a family does not derive its sense of worth from being told by the state, "You're married, congratulations!" The sense of family comes from the commitment we make to one another to work through the hard times so we can enjoy the good ones. It comes from the love that binds us. That's what makes a family.

As I watched the 2004 GOP convention unfold, I realized that preventing parents like mine from being married was what they meant when they said "protect marriage" and "protect family values." Every speaker used those two phrases. They each talked about how vital it was to secure and protect the bonds of matrimony, as though they were borders under siege from the gay scourge. I noted the following quote from then–Pennsylvania Senator Rick Santorum:

"Karen, my incredible wife and mother of our six children, always says, 'Rick, the best gift we can give our kids is a great marriage. It gives them the security they want and the example they need.'"

That's exactly what Terry and Jackie have given each other and given Zebby and me for our formative years. To suggest otherwise is factually incorrect. I was perplexed as to why Senator Santorum would want to deprive a family like mine of both the security and the example that he seemed to think were so important. Did he simply think my family was somehow worth less than his own? That we shouldn't exist?

It wasn't the last time America would hear from Mr. Santorum. Even after he was voted out of office by a seventeen-point margin, he left the U.S. Senate and remained an outspoken advocate against same-sex marriage, writing two books and numerous articles about the topic. In college, my freshman rhetoric class assessed one of Mr. Santorum's essays about the alleged public health risks of legalizing same-sex marriage. Despite professing to be an objective, rational defense of "traditional" marriage, his argument was riddled with logical and rhetorical fallacies, including the ludicrous claim that homosexuality causes HIV/AIDS.

"Well, sure, but that's kind of a ridiculous argument," said Max, one of my fellow classmates. "Being gay doesn't cause HIV/AIDS. Unsafe sex with somebody who has HIV/AIDS does."

"But gay people have lots of unsafe sex," replied another. "That's just a fact."

I kept my mouth shut.

"You're telling a college class that only gay people have unsafe sex?" replied Max. Most of us laughed. It was a pretty ridiculous statement, considering that, according to a 2008 Centers for Disease Control (CDC) study, one out of four teenage girls has contracted a sexually transmitted infection (STI).

This public health contention is actually a really common argument used in the same-sex marriage debate. It's also a classic example of poor argumentation, something I often encountered during my years as a high school debater—the confusion of causation and correlation. Causation is a direct relationship in which A causes B. Correlation is an indirect relationship in which A and B are often seen together.

Here's an example: Factually speaking, it was about the

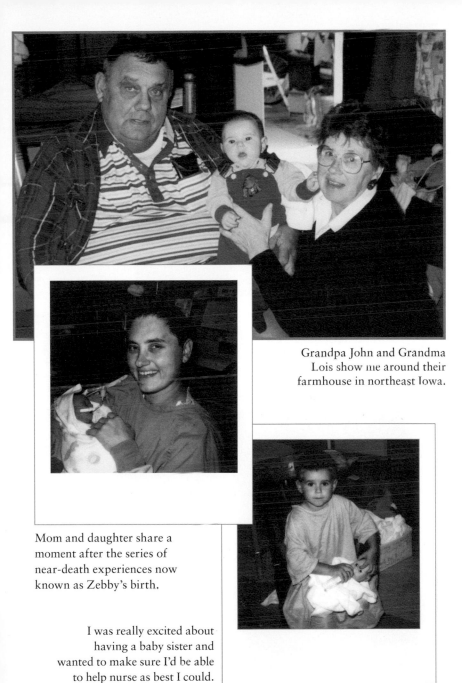

Grandpa John and Grandma Lois show me around their farmhouse in northeast Iowa.

Mom and daughter share a moment after the series of near-death experiences now known as Zebby's birth.

I was really excited about having a baby sister and wanted to make sure I'd be able to help nurse as best I could.

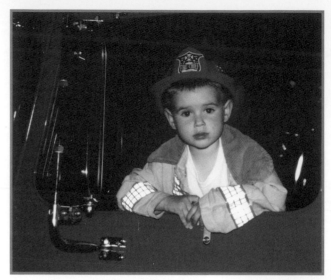

I think I was a firefighter for Halloween my first four or five Halloweens.

Zebby and I chill out on my favorite beanbag chair as I undergo the lengthy healing process required to mend my fractured femur.

I really liked that hat.

Andy, my best friend in Wisconsin, is the guy holding the huge trophy. Although the Batmobile may not have finished in first place, it did win Best Paint and Design. I'll take what I can get.

My moms like to joke that I've always been full of hot air.

My troop prepares to venture off to my first official Boy Scouts summer camp.

Family portrait after my moms' first commitment ceremony.

I wait, with nervous anticipation, to be called in for my Eagle Scout Board of Review, the final step of a long, long journey.

The Eagle Scout Court of Honor tracks my progression from short to tall and Tenderfoot to Eagle.

In July 2005, as Terry's physical condition began its rapid descent, she had to succumb to life in a wheelchair. Even as her future darkened, she found bright moments during our annual visits to a UU family summer camp.

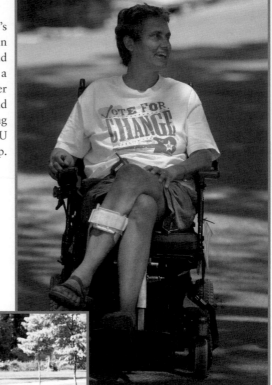

This picture was taken in October of 2008, slightly less than a year after Terry began her new physical therapy and intensive nutrition protocols.

Jackie and I pose on the edge of the Grand Canyon
on the first day of our weeklong mountain biking trip with the
Adventure Bus through Arizona and Utah.

Jackie conquers the West.

My moms exchange their vows (and rings) for the third time as Sara Wahls, Terry's cousin, and her partner, Kim, watch.

After making it through the trials of multiple sclerosis, social disenfranchisement, and legal discrimination, the brides share their first kiss as a legally wedded couple.

time pirates slowly began vanishing from the seas that the average global temperature slowly began to rise. Did the eradication of pirates lead to global warming? Obviously not. But there is an undeniable correlation between the average global temperature and a lack of eye patch–wearing, cutlass-wielding, rum-drinking pirates.

Being gay doesn't cause HIV. You'll notice that neither of my moms, two "avowed" homosexuals, ever came down with it. However, based on certain tendencies and characteristics of gay culture here in the U.S., many gay men put themselves in situations where contracting HIV/AIDS is more likely than it would be in other situations that require the use of contraception to prevent pregnancy as well as the spread of STIs. This is also the case for many African men and women, many of whom frequently engage in anal sex because they lack access to birth control and other contraceptive technologies. Though anal sex has a higher STI-transmission rate than penile-vaginal intercourse, it is by no means practiced exclusively by gay people.

"So then what?" the other student replied. "Anyone can get married? If being of the opposite sex doesn't matter, then any two people could just get married for the tax benefits and stuff."

"Um, that's already the case for straight people, dude," said Max.

"Oh. Yeah." Pause. "I mean, I guess so." Another pause. "What about the kids, though? His study is really clear about that."

And the study certainly seemed to be clear. Kids who grew up in a household with a mom and a dad were much more likely to achieve success later in life. They were more likely to attend college, less likely to go to jail, more likely to have higher incomes, more likely to get married, less likely to get divorced, and had, on average, longer life spans.

Max didn't have a witty comeback for this one, and silence began to settle.

I cut it short.

"No, his study isn't clear about it at all," I interjected. "In fact, it's exactly like the HIV/AIDs thing. He didn't establish causation, there's no link." I tried to make sure that I didn't slip any further into the übertechnical debate jargon I had picked up in high school. "It's not an apples-to-apples comparison. He's not comparing kids with two moms or two dads to kids with one mom and one dad; he's comparing kids with only one parent to kids with both a mom and a dad."

I looked around the classroom and could tell that my explanation wasn't clear.

"I have two gay moms. I promise you that my family situation was much closer to growing up with both a mom and a dad than growing up with only one parent. And even then, my girlfriend was raised by a single mother, and she's a Presidential Scholar. She's doing just fine. This study isn't actually about parents; it's about income level. Low-income families are much more likely than high-income families to have only one parent in the home, that's what this study is about, and obviously kids from high-income families are going to lead more 'successful' lives, whatever that means."

This was resonating.

"And Rick Santorum knew that when he wrote this article. This is intellectually dishonest, pure and simple," I finished. I didn't say or observe this at the time, but I'm certainly of the opinion that making intellectually dishonest arguments— as many advocates on the other side of this message routinely do—is not respectful, and it is certainly not courteous. Such blatant intellectual dishonesty is presumptuous, insulting, and shows a lack of respect for the electorate. When any politician gets on his or her soapbox and abuses the power and authority that comes with that position, he or she embodies the politics of fear. Such practices might make for good short-term results or raise a lot of campaign money from people terrified by the "homosexual agenda," but such arguments are not becoming of the people we elect to represent and protect the interests of *all* Americans.

By the time I was in college reviewing Mr. Santorum's writings, I had four years of high school debate training and coaching under my belt. Back in eighth grade, I was not so fortunate. I remember going back into class the day after the convention and reading through my list of grievances without explaining why this issue was so personally frustrating. Looking back, I'm sure my teacher knew exactly why. (I somehow failed to realize the obvious, that Jackie and Terry took turns going to parent-teacher conferences.) He didn't seem to care about my motivations, however, and was far more interested in what I thought were the problems with the speakers' arguments, namely that they didn't really draw on any evidence to support their claims.

"They're all saying that children deserve a mother and a father, but they don't say why," I said. "They kept saying that marriage is only between a woman and a man but don't explain why."

"Okay, Zach," my teacher said, "that's a good point, but do they really have to explain why? These speeches aren't very long, and they don't have a whole lot of time."

"I don't think you should be allowed to just say something like that without explaining why you're saying it," I protested. "It's just . . . wrong."

I thought to myself, *We are a family. We do have values. We work on them every night. We live them every day. I'm in Boy Scouts.*

The GOP convention was another example of a time when people tried to convince me that my family was different, and I should feel that something was out of order. Though I never had a dad, I have never felt a void in my life. I never felt like there was a missing piece. Whatever absence there may have been was seamlessly filled by the love of my family and friends.

But the people speaking out against my family didn't know that. They never bothered to ask me what I thought—they never bothered to ask any of us. They just presumed away the normalcy of our lives and arrived, without evidence, at the conclusion that my sister and I—and millions of kids with families like ours—were somehow worse off than their own children *because* our parents were gay. More troubling is that they stood up in support of divisive policies without even having the courage to call their actions what they were: discrimination. Instead, claiming the mantle of moral superiority, they rode off into battle to defend America's families from the ultimate enemy: other American families.

THE MERITS OF COURTESY

In my family, we have a simple rule when it comes to dinner-table manners: If you say "yuck," you get a second helping. Call it Midwestern folksiness, just being polite, or whatever you'd like, but my moms never ceased in their efforts to raise a gentleman. They both knew what if felt like to be disrespected, sometimes egregiously so, and wanted to make sure that their son would treat others with the respect and decency all people deserve. In Scouts we learned *"A Scout is polite regardless of age or position. He knows good manners make it easier for people to get along together."*

Kindness is having good intentions for others. Courtesy is taking that a step further and making it happen. Courtesy is considering the consequences of your actions and how what you do and say will affect others. Courtesy in a movie theater is putting your cell phone on silent or, even better, shutting it off completely. Courtesy in politics is resisting the urge to engage in name-calling and refusing to blindly deny that a family you never met can make a positive contribution to society.

In situations small or large, courtesy is a combination of respecting the experience of others and taking responsibility for your actions by recognizing the power you have to affect the lives of those around you.

I watched as others afforded my family courtesies during the worst of Terry's MS—an expedited journey through airport security, opening a door as Terry rumbled up in her wheelchair, offering a seat so she didn't have to stand—each time appreciating the generosity of strangers and knowing that I had an obligation to pay such courtesy forward. Nobody ever asked about the sexuality of the woman in the wheelchair.

My roommate during my sophomore year of college was a guy by the name of Brandon Pearson. Brandon is from a small town near Cedar Rapids, about an hour north of where I grew up in Iowa City. He's a conservative Christian, a committed Lutheran who goes to church every Sunday with his equally reverent girlfriend of three years. When we were living together, he was finishing his senior year at Iowa, planning to graduate with an integrated physiology major and then go on to study chiropractic therapy.

Brandon and I were both pretty big into fitness, and we spent a lot of time in the gym together. We would get up around five every morning to make omelets and protein shakes before heading out to the rec center at about six. On the bus ride in and while we were lifting, we often shot the bull about our political and philosophical differences. I was always shocked by how much our views overlapped. Even though we usually took markedly different routes, we often arrived at the same conclusion. When it came to same-sex marriage, he didn't have a problem with it.

"Yeah, I believe that homosexuality is a sin," he told me one morning. "But we're all sinners. And as long as it isn't harming anyone else, I don't see what the big deal is."

Clearly I don't think that homosexuality is a sin, but I can respect Brandon's point of view. More to the point, I think Brandon's guiding philosophy—as long as it doesn't hurt anybody it shouldn't be illegal—is spot on.

That's just common courtesy.

CHAPTER 9

Cheerful

A chemo cycle is essentially a race, a bet in which the odds are never known for sure and you can only pray that they're in your favor. You're hooked up to an IV, and the chemo drips into your bloodstream. But, even though you're sitting in a hospital and being attended to by a nurse, the chemo flowing into your body isn't medicine—it's poison. The hope is to starve the disease of the resources it needs to continue replicating, without killing the host: you. The race is between a dying disease and a dying patient, and the winner takes all.

Jackie sat Zebby and me down, once again armed with professional-looking brochures, to explain the changes that were going to happen. Terry would be even weaker than usual. There was a good chance that some of her hair would fall out. She was going to be spending most of her time alone in the master bedroom, and if we wanted to see her, we would have to take care not to sneeze or cough. Her immune system would be badly weakened from fighting both MS *and* the chemo.

She had to take an entire week off from work to recover from the first round. She was in bed for more than twenty hours a day, with the drapes pulled and lights off. I came down with a stomachache halfway through the week and was sent off to stay with Nic because there was an off chance that I had the flu. With the state that Terry's immune system was in, something as mild as the common cold would have been dangerous—influenza would have been deadly.

After finishing the horrible chemo cycles, Terry's MS symptoms were still as bad as ever, maybe worse. The pain that she had endured for weeks and weeks had done absolutely nothing to abate the disease. Though she'd didn't lose the race, which is to say she hadn't died, MS had won, because in many ways she was even further behind than when she started.

We were in the middle of a storm, but nobody wanted to talk about the weather.

My mom started stumbling more. Falling was a constant concern, and she was increasingly fragile. I took the precaution of putting the gate we had used while training our dog back in its place in front of the stairwell—an accidental fall could be fatal. At dinner Terry would sometimes drop her plate, spilling food across the table, unable to even lift a ladle full of soup.

Jackie and I would exchange looks before shuffling to clean up the mess.

A lot was said, but nothing was spoken.

And somehow, bless her, my mom would find something to smile about. She'd tell a bad joke (almost all of her jokes are) or share, for the thousandth time, a story that had once been funny. Here she was, the subject of so much pain and pressure and worry, and she found herself playing the part of cheerleader, even though she was the one in the wheelchair.

I'm occasionally asked how I learned about values like courage and self-discipline and perseverance "without a dad." I usually respond to whomever is asking by saying that clearly he doesn't know much about the women in his life. I've never been asked this question by a woman.

Even though my moms had never been big into watching lots of TV or movies when my sister and I were younger, as Terry's mobility waned, watching movies became one of the few activities we could do as a family without testing Terry's strength. Uncharacteristically, they bought a new, flat-screen TV and put it in their room, so we'd be able to have family movie nights without having to go down to the basement where we kept our other TV.

Instead of approaching these family movie nights with a bad attitude—resigning ourselves to what we knew was one of the only things we could do together as a family—we brought a good mind to the evenings, breaking out popcorn, apples, cheese, and root beer. What could have been macabre reminders of how few options we had left, we made into fulfilling experiences.

It amazed me how my mom always kept a positive attitude, even in the face of such a terrifying disease. Of course, positive didn't always mean happy. There were plenty of nights when staying positive pretty much meant we got through dinner without our conversations about grades and homework and sports not devolving into a shouting match.

Even though Terry would sometimes laugh at what seemed to be the most inappropriate moments, and I would roll my eyes, exasperated by yet *another* bad joke, she'd wind up having the last laugh when—despite the medical community's long-held belief that MS leads down a one-way road of relentless decline—she willed herself out of the wheelchair.

For spring break during my freshman year of high school, we decided to visit my mom's brother Denis and his family down in St. Petersburg, Florida. We knew that the beaches of Florida might be our last family vacation, but none of us were saying that. We just focused on getting there.

When we traveled long distances, we brought a special folding, tilt-recline wheelchair for my mom to use, because her electric tilt-recline wheelchair was too bulky to fit on the plane. We had a super-short connection time between our flights, so we didn't check any bags. As soon as her special wheelchair was unloaded, I quickly unfolded it and set it up— an action that was second nature by this point. Terry limped to the chair, I strapped her in and reclined it, taking the stress off her back. We put a couple bags on her lap—she didn't mind—and then we pretty much sprinted to the next gate. We must have looked a little ridiculous.

While on the trip in Florida, we spent a memorable afternoon kayaking on the bay in a beautiful, lush inlet not too far from Denis's house. It was tough getting my mom in the kayak without tipping it over, but we managed to get her in the boat and set out onto the water.

Mom and I were in one kayak, Jackie and Zebby were in another one far ahead of us. Although Terry had been the one to teach me how to kayak, now she could barely paddle. It was my time to be the navigator, the stronger person in the back doing the lion's share of the work and steering our course.

Even though it was a calm day, I felt my heart racing. Not from the excitement or the exercise, but from the question that continued to float around in the back of my mind.

The conversation finally turned to her MS. Her illness was still a changing, unknown factor in all our lives, and none of us were sure what was going to happen next. I needed to know more about it. I'd read on the Internet that in some cases MS was terminal, causing an "early death." And I very clearly knew what that meant.

When I was younger, misery seemed to come knocking every time there was something to celebrate: Grandpa John died on my second birthday. My mom almost died giving birth to Zebby. I broke my leg on my third Christmas. Grandma Lois had a heart attack two days before my fourth birthday. Needless to say, I was pretty nervous every time a holiday rolled around.

It was not too long after I turned four that the notion of death sunk in. I suddenly understood the finality of death, and I remember running into my mom's room, exclaiming that I didn't want her to die. There were tears.

Around that time, Terry bought a book by Leo Buscaglia called *The Fall of Freddie the Leaf*. It's a simple story about a maple leaf named Freddie who, along with his fellow leaves, experiences the passing of the seasons, from his birth in spring to his death in winter. He befriends a larger leaf named Daniel, who has a deeper understanding of life and death and explains that death is about letting go. At the end, he understands that death is a part of life and falls to the ground with the winter snow.

The metaphor helped me to understand, if not accept, that life has different phases. In the book, each leaf leaves the tree differently. Some leaves fiercely battle against the wind, while others drift down quietly. Freddie resists until he is the last leaf on the branch, brown and withered. When he finally lets go, he achieves a great peace. The simple story and beautiful pictures eloquently explained that we all go.

But even so, the thought of my mom's death had become a constant, private worry.

I was growing frustrated by her memory loss, and though she never said anything to us, I think she was, too. As head of the household, she didn't want that to be true, couldn't let that be true. But it was frustrating as an adolescent boy to be told I could do something like spend time with friends, and then come home to her railing at me with, "Zach, where were you? Why didn't you tell me?" I wanted to scream, "I did!" but knowing she was the authority and was herself increasingly bothered by her predicament, I knew that wasn't going to fly. I wasn't going to say, "Hey, Mom, it's your MS. Your memory is going."

As we glided along in the water, I was still trying to understand what this all meant for my family. I could see that my mom's strength was sapped. She was pretending to paddle, but she wasn't really helping. The doctor in her clearly knew all about the effects and possibilities of her disease. Was she also pretending that she wasn't scared in order to protect us?

I forget how the topic actually came up, but the conversation came around to her diagnosis. "Aren't you scared of MS, you know . . . killing you?" I asked.

I couldn't see her face because she was sitting in the front of the kayak, and we were both facing forward. She didn't really say anything right away. Then she slowly turned around and looked at me. I stopped paddling, and our kayak glided to a stop.

"Well, no, I'm not," she said. "I've been lucky enough to have been blessed with this incredible family, to have you and Zebby, and Jackie as my wife. I've loved. And, honestly, at this point, I'm not afraid of death."

I couldn't understand that. She had so much to lose. She had us to lose! It wasn't just about losing her strength; she stood to lose her family, her life. Unlike her, I was very much afraid of death. In a lot of ways, I still am. I forget where I read this, but it still rings true: "Everyone wants to go to heaven, but no one wants to die."

Later, in some of my angsty high school journaling, while trying to cope with the reality of my mom's diagnosis, I would write:

> If you were to live forever, life would become meaningless. Knowing that you have only one shot gives that attempt so much value. It's knowing that you will only see a finite number of beautiful, heartbreakingly beautiful, sunsets that gives each sunset the power to paralyze you.

I don't know if I meant it then, or truly believe it now, but it's what I told myself over and over when I was trying to get through the days.

"Look, Zach, I've lived, really lived," my mom told me. "It's been great. I'm not rushing to die, clearly, but if that's what's going to happen . . ." she trailed off. And then softly and with great weight behind her words said, "You can't let fear of death dictate your life."

Without responding, I looked out at the water. I didn't care if she was fine with it or not—I wasn't.

There wasn't a whole lot more to say. Even though the conversation had not been long, it was one of the few, direct talks we had about her MS. Unable to bring myself to discuss the topic further, I turned to writing, starting a blog on Xanga to house my thoughts.

The following was one of my first entries:

The Prison
"I'm sorry, Doctor. The test results were positive."

Her whole world goes reeling. A wave of nausea rushes up her chest into her head.

She sits.

"We can't determine how quickly it will progress, it varies from case to case."

This can't be happening. She's dreaming, she knows it.

"There are things you can do. But there's no denying it, your ability to walk, even to move will be limited."

A groan of frustration escapes her. What else can

she do? Just when life was picking up too. Visions of kayaking, hiking, and mountain climbing fade away. Dreams of spending time with her kids, biking, playing, and running, all gone.

"You're going to wind up in a wheelchair, and unfortunately, it's only a matter of time."

And this is the worst. Not, "You're going to be in a wheelchair now," but instead it's a "matter of time." Time that will be spent slowly watching her strength be leeched from her body. Time that will be spent watching herself waste away, despite her best efforts to the contrary. Time that will be spent lying to her children about a future their family won't have.

"As you know, there are two types, one that affects the brain, the other the spinal cord. As you know, it has attacked your spinal cord."

Instead of losing her cognitive capacity, it is her motor functions that will be sacrificed. She will be completely conscious of her waning physical abilities, instead of being blissfully ignorant of her deteriorating mental condition.

"And I also regret to inform you that at this time there are no cures. Only treatments. There are several things that you can do. . . ."

She tunes him out. He continues as though he knows more about her ailment than she. Hah. She had researched exhaustively. She knew the symptoms. The exhaustion. The sore back. The fatigue. And of course, the pain. Not just regular migraines.

No, *this was much worse. Try to imagine somebody peeling the skin off your face. Then multiply that pain times ten. That would get you pretty close. The "zingers" as she refers to them. Something that she fears more than death.*

She looks back up at the young doctor, who is not the judge. Not the jury. Not the executioner. He's simply reading her sentence. Which, of course, is one for life. She raises her hands and looks at them. No, she is her own jailer. The executioner lies within her, attacking the nerves in her legs and lower back, creating a prison worse than any maximum security federal penitentiary.

Her crime? Living.

Her sentence? Loss of movement and eventually death.

Her executioner? Multiple sclerosis.

Her prison?

She laughs darkly, stands up and walks away.

THE MERITS OF CHEERFULNESS

"A Scout looks for the bright side of things. He cheerfully does tasks that come his way. He tries to make others happy." Cheerfulness is internally motivated. It's rooted in an acknowledgment that life will not always break your way and that sometimes we all have to do things that we don't want to do and endure things that are hard to endure. There's a certain humility that precedes this understanding, and I often think of the prayer, "God give me the courage to change what I can, the serenity to accept the things I cannot, and the wisdom, always, to know the difference." There's a level of self-confidence, too, that's required, a faith in one's ability to effect change. Otherwise you have to resign your life to merely being a supporting role in somebody else's show.

And I think it was that last ingredient that I was missing for a long time.

At the beginning of eighth grade, I enrolled in an Honors Leadership seminar. Of course, leadership in junior high pretty much just means planning the school dances, which is exactly what we did. By the end of the first trimester, though, I thought that the system used to design the dances could be vastly improved, and I decided to run for vice president of the student body. If you remember anything about junior high, you'll probably remember that such elections are usually little more than popularity contests, and I was a *long* ways away from popular.

But before I could even get to the election, I had to gather up enough signatures to get my name on the ballot. Talking with my friends over lunch, and then their other friends, I managed to get more than twice what was needed. Great success. And campaigning basically came down to a short speech by each candidate that all students would watch in their first-period classes on the school's closed-circuit TV system.

The morning we would be delivering the speeches, I remember getting my books out of my locker when a fellow candidate, one of the popular girls—and, as always, her entourage—sauntered up to her own locker. I don't remember exactly what was said, but they seemed awfully confident in her inevitable victory.

Turns out they shouldn't have been.

I'm not sure what the final vote count wound up being, but I walked out of the building that day as the vice president–elect. Kind of had a ring to it. Mine would be a pretty successful term. We got the administration to allow snowboarding at our annual ski trip to a local mountain—or as mountainous as hills get in Iowa—and solidified the tradition of keeping the eighth-grade formal dance free to all students.

My mom often reflects that I started to really find my stride in eighth grade, and I think being elected by my peers to a leadership position—even one as corny as vice president of a junior high student body—was a big part of that. It became a source of confidence for me, a confidence that played a major role in my effort to bounce back from the ceaseless, eroding struggles we often faced as we dealt with the reality of Terry's MS.

What began as a burgeoning confidence, however, quickly developed into an outward personality of false bravado that was often interpreted as arrogance. The longer I wore that cowl of confidence, the more I started to believe it myself. Kurt Vonnegut once observed that we are who we pretend to be, so we should be careful who we pretend to be.

This goes both ways. On the one hand, I know that all too often Terry's outward cheerfulness was an attempt to "fake it till you make it," and that wound up keeping our family afloat. On the other, what was my way of propping myself up was sometimes misinterpreted as cockiness. In an effort to conquer both a discomfort of the present and fear for the future, I had found solace in bravado.

By the time I was finishing my junior year of high school, my mom's MS symptoms were slowly abating. I was performing at a high level in speech and debate and had achieved the highest rank in Boy Scouts. My false sense of outward confidence gave way to a well-rooted belief in my ability to actually deal with the task at hand and to positively shape my situation.

To this day I've maintained a constructive outlook on life, but I've also learned that a little humility goes a long way. I might have been a bit of a cocky pain in the ass for a while, but I think (or hope) that that bravado has matured into a genuine cheerfulness and sincere respect that I try to maintain in my approach to the world.

I've learned that cheerfulness is the mind-set you bring to any given task, be it homework, chores, your profession, your love life, or your family life. Cheerfulness, just like misery, is infectious. Sure it's easier to be cheerful on a sunny day than it is on a gray day, and as we worked through the challenges facing our family we didn't need to lean on one another for support on the good days. We could rely on ourselves. On the bad days, however, we needed one another's support and loyalty to our family as a whole. As I observed in my testimony, we worked through the hard times so we could enjoy the good ones.

The bottom line is that when it comes to being cheerful, external validation is a poor substitute for internal faith. The validation I received in eighth grade when I was elected vice president felt amazing, but it was both fickle and fleeting and proved to be a poor foundation when I wasn't elected to a second term.

I felt a similar feeling in the immediate wake of my testimony going viral. As the praise and congratulations poured in, I felt both overwhelmed and intoxicated. The debater in me felt as though he had just won a national championship with a perfect ballot, awash in the thrill of winning a high-stakes competition.

But I now have the sensibility to know that as nice as the accolades feel, they cannot serve as a foundation in and of themselves. Far more important is what led me to deliver the testimony in the first place: loyalty to family, duty to a cause greater than myself, faith in my ability to perform when it matters most, and a confidence that told me no matter what happened in that hearing, I was doing my part to advance the cause of love and justice.

It would take deliberate effort not to be cheerful about that.

CHAPTER 10

Loyal

When Terry's health was slipping further and further away, sometimes I couldn't help but wonder why Jackie stuck around. It wasn't that I didn't understand what love or loyalty or commitment were—even though I was only at the beginning of adolescence, I knew enough about these values to understand that they were important and that Terry, Jackie, Zebby, and I all shared them.

What I didn't understand was why Jackie was willing to risk suffering through an extended illness and then losing the person she loved on terms that weren't her own. She could have decided to walk away from the situation on her own terms when she learned of Terry's diagnosis back in 2000, and I'm not sure anyone would have blamed her. She would have been violating her "in sickness and in health" commitment to Terry, yet I don't think I would have said that she was in the wrong. Disrespectful, maybe, but not morally repugnant.

But she didn't.

And further, if she'd lost Terry, she would have lost Zebby and me, too. The mother of a close friend of mine remembers my expressing concern when I was fourteen about what would happen to Zebby and me if Terry's illness became fully debilitating or if her face pain pushed her into a coma. Even though we'd been living together for nearly a decade, Jackie didn't have parental custody rights. In fact, when it came to our family, she didn't have any rights at all—a reality I had witnessed firsthand in the lead-up to our relocation to Iowa.

During one of our first visits to Iowa City, while Mom went through a series of job interviews, Jackie kept Zebby and me distracted at the hotel. Zebby, then six years old, fell while jumping back and forth between the two beds and hurt her arm. The nurse in Jackie knew it was serious and quickly put us in the car and headed to the nearby University of Iowa Hospital.

Zebby had broken her arm, but because Jackie wasn't Zebby's "real" mother, the hospital had to get Terry's approval on any course of treatment. As my sister cried and endured the pain, the hospital administrator attempted to track Terry down. In the meantime, Jackie bribed Zebby into obeying the doctors by using a supply of Pokémon cards she had in her bag. Zebby got one card each time she did what the doctors asked. Even though she knew Zebby, knew how to get her to cooperate, and as a nurse knew what needed to be done, to the hospital she wasn't qualified to make any decisions. She was little more than a glorified babysitter.

When it happened, I didn't fully understand why that had been the case or what the implications were, but by the time I was starting to really worry about Terry's health, I knew that Jackie had zero legal obligation to stick around. I mean, they weren't even married, which, according to the politicians on TV, was the "ultimate" commitment. There was nothing standing in her path if she chose to run.

But she stayed. She knew a little something about loyalty.

Grandpa Eugene, Jackie's dad, had been diagnosed with Parkinson's disease in the early '90s and had deteriorated rapidly. He had been a decorated lightweight boxer in high school, and Jackie knew that those intense years had likely left a mark of permanent damage. Parkinson's disease, like multiple sclerosis, is a neurodegenerative disorder that often leads to decreased motor ability, speech impediments, cognitive dysfunction, dementia, and other neuropsychiatric problems. Parkinson's, like MS, has no officially recognized cure, only treatments that delay the inevitable.

But Grandma Esther, Jackie's mom, didn't have time for the inevitable and worked relentlessly to secure Grandpa Eugene's well-being and provide him with the most comfortable livelihood she could give him. Her fridge was always stocked with 7UP and A&W Root Beer, Eugene's favorite sodas. She signed Christmas and birthday cards "Esther and Eugene" long after he lost the ability to write. She was at his side when he passed.

When I met Eugene, he could barely say my name, although the spark in his eyes and the softest hints of a smile communicated what his voice could not. By the time he died, he could no longer form complete words, lacking both the physical and mental capacity to do so. Looking back, there's no doubt in my mind that Jackie saw parallels between the hell her father lived in and the future awaiting the woman she loved. They were simply too obvious to miss.

I'm sure Terry saw them, too.

I tried to figure out why Jackie was staying, why she wasn't scared of losing Terry like she had lost her father. It was only later that I realized she was scared—she was terrified. She had watched her father wither into a shell of the man he used to be, confined by the fetters of an incurable neurodegenerative disease, despite the sincerest efforts of Jackie and her mother to fight it. The incredible mix of loyalty, courage, and foolishness that we call love triumphed over fear, and the Reger-Wahls family remained intact.

And now, as Grandma Esther grows older (a great-grandmother twice over already!), Jackie has been the one to stand by her side and support her through heart failure, strokes, and major surgery, even as she continues to question the legitimacy of her only daughter's family. Amid a slew of problems involving bankruptcy, a pair of nasty divorces that left the family divided, and Eugene's passing, Jackie has remained a rock of support in Esther's life.

To me, in some ways, that loyalty is even more telling than Jackie's refusal to abandon Terry during the worst of her MS. Unlike the rest of Jackie's family, we were located nearly six hours away from her mom, who still lived in Wausau, Wisconsin. If Jackie had wanted to, cutting the ties would have been well within the realm of possibility. But she didn't. That's not who she is.

Because I see so many similarities in character between

Jackie and Terry, I have never questioned Jackie's legitimacy as a mom. I don't have any recollection of ever pulling the you're-not-my-real-mom card on her. When I called her to double-check, she didn't remember any instances of that, either, but joked that if I had, she would have caned me. We laughed, and that was that.

Loyalty is sometimes as simple as standing by the people you love.

My Eagle Scout ceremony was held on a cold Monday night in early March 2007. A lot of Eagles look back and reflect that obtaining that rank is more important than graduating from high school, and I would agree. My family had invited many friends and all our family to the event. Scattered throughout the audience were many of my mentors, former teachers, and those close to our family. And my moms were there, something about which I didn't even think twice, though my moms had thought about it for weeks.

There was a bunch of my memorabilia on display. Tanna, our babysitter/nanny had helped to set everything up, as Terry was still resting and Jackie was ushering friends and family around. Laid out neatly on a large table were my old Cub Scout uniform, my Pinewood Derby car (the award-winning Batmobile!), and lots of pictures.

Getting an Eagle Scout award is a Big Deal. To my knowledge, the fact that I had two moms was not a big deal to anyone involved in my troop or the Scouting community. The big deal to me was that we had to bring along the zero-grav chair. Unbeknownst to me, my mom had spent the entire day leading up to the ceremony resting, hoping she would be able to stand for the part of the ceremony she would share with Jackie and me.

After handing out a series of other awards and recognitions for the last few months of merit badge work, it was my time. The national BSA organization has a prewritten script for the way the ceremony is supposed to unfold, although they are more "guidelines" than actual rules, and my moms had made some creative changes to the script.

The ceremony began with an invocation from Nancy Hailey, our minister at the Unitarian Universalist church. Our Scoutmaster said a few words, and then Nic's dad, Larry, took the floor to deliver his remarks, making a few jokes and presenting me as a Scout of good character. After that we moved on to lighting candles that represented each rank earned, and reading aloud descriptions of each rank. In slightly unorthodox fashion, my moms recruited a bunch of younger boys to represent my various stops along the journey to Eagle. One person represented my time in Cub Scouts, and there was one guy for each Boy Scout rank, from Tenderfoot through Life. Instead of the senior patrol leader reading each description, as is usually the case, each version of my younger (and shorter) self—my moms put them in order based on their heights— read a description of the rank. My moms made sure the little guys had the shortest sentences.

Looking toward the ceremony from my seat in the audience, the presentation was a wonderful visual illustration of my years in Scouts and gave me a moment of pause as I reflected on how much I had matured and learned as a result of the time I had spent in the organization.

In addition to the aesthetic enhancements, there was another obvious change to the script they had needed to make: how to handle the pin ceremony that was yet to come.

The standard script from the national BSA includes the following passage:

> *Your father has stood by you over the years and has offered his encouragement and assistance, as the symbol of what he has contributed to your attainment of this award, the court now asks you to present him a miniature Eagle tie tack.*

Clearly we were going to have to make some adjustments. The real question was whether both moms would be able to stand by me as their awards were presented and I was recognized.

After the lighting ceremony, our Scoutmaster, Clark Zarafis, then delivered the Eagle Scout charge:

> *I charge you to undertake your citizenship with a solemn dedication. Be a leader, but lead only toward the best. Lift up every task you do and every office you hold to the high level of service to God and your fellow man—to finest living. We have too many who use their strength and their intellect to exploit others for selfish gains. . . . I charge you to be among those who dedicate their skills and ability to the common good. Build America on the solid foundation of clean living, honest work, unselfish citizenship, and reverence for*

> *God; and whatever others may do, you will leave be-*
> *hind you a record of which every Scout may be proud.*

With those final words, the Eagle honor guard stood up. Jackie stood as well and reached down to help Terry slowly ease out of her chair. As I watched my mom start to stand, I realized that for the entire ceremony she hadn't been able to see anything. She had been looking up at the ceiling, which was why she had been so keen on having Zebby take a lot of pictures. Being reclined had prevented her from witnessing the scene she had worked so hard to create.

Slowly but surely, she found her footing. The honor guard walked my two moms to the front of the room, where Terry steadied herself with two canes, looking gray and ashen. Knowing she could only stand for a few minutes, the honor guard quickly tied the new neckerchief to my current one and then slid it around my neck, so as to symbolically never break the chain of Scouting. They then secured the neckerchief with a new slide and shook my hand, welcoming me to the brotherhood of Eagle.

The Scoutmaster read aloud the revised passage, acknowledging my family's configuration, and I fastened the heart-shaped pins to my moms' jackets.

Mitt Romney once wrote that it's the mothers who make the Eagles, and as my two moms stood there with me, tears spilling down their faces, I grasped just how full circle this moment was. They had stood with me throughout my journey, loyally supporting and encouraging me when I needed it most.

But in that moment—our moment—I was incredibly proud that we got to stand together for just a little bit longer.

THE MERITS OF LOYALTY

When I'm out on the speaking circuit, the people who attend my talks are sometimes surprised by my passionate loyalty to the Green Bay Packers. (A boy who was raised by two moms loves football?!) I still remember the elation of watching the Packers crush the New England Patriots in Super Bowl XXXI when I was almost six years old and then feeling distraught the following year when John Elway's Denver Broncos beat back the Pack's effort to repeat as Super Bowl champs. I asked my moms if this meant that we had to start rooting for the Broncos. They chuckled and told me no, we didn't have to do that. People don't walk away from sports teams just because they lose, and there's something powerful in sticking with your team—the victories are that much sweeter.

At a recent speech in central Wisconsin, I referenced my years as a quarterback in high school and was asked during a Q&A if my moms had been the ones to introduce me to football. They were indeed. And I'll never forget watching the gears turn behind the eyes of the guy who asked, a man in his mid-twenties wearing leather work boots, a baseball cap, and a well-worn pair of blue jeans. He seemed baffled to learn that the homosexual "lifestyle choice" occasionally includes putting on a cheese head and curling up with a beer on the couch to watch some Green Bay Packers football.

While I'd been going through the talk, this man's reactions and facial expressions had suggested strong skepticism of my story and my upbringing, and he was probably only attending my lecture at all because his sociology professor had assigned it. I thought it remarkable that this man was so dumbfounded by the fact that he shared this love of, and loyalty to, a pro-football team with my moms.

As he struggled to wrap his mind around the fact that my moms love football, maybe he realized that when the camera pans across the crowd watching a game at Lambeau Field, the gay people in attendance aren't blurred out or painted blue. Amid the cheese heads, face paint, Aaron Rodgers jerseys, and sea of green and yellow, they're completely indistinguishable from everyone else.

There must have been something incredibly humanizing, too, about learning of this shared admiration. Without even meeting my moms, this guy bonded with them over their shared love of the Green Bay Packers. It might seem foreign or strange to someone who doesn't follow the game, but speaking as a guy who grew up in a part of the country where the Packers game was Sunday's second sermon, I can attest to the power of such loyalty. The importance of loyalty was such a big component of my Scouting experience: "*A Scout is true to his family, Scout leaders, friends, school, and nation.*"

When my mom was at her worst, I remember walking in the door one night and Jackie immediately put her finger to her mouth and said, "Shh!"

"What's going on?" I asked.

"Mom's zingers are back."

I felt my stomach drop. Despite her declining stamina, she hadn't had a bad episode of face pain in almost a year, something we had all been grateful for, but now they were back with a vengeance. I made my way to the master bedroom, where the blinds were down, the curtains were drawn, and the lights were off. I knelt by the bed, worked my hand into my mom's and squeezed. Her eyes were shut, but she was not sleeping. Her chin was shaking and her head softly rocked as she silently tried to work through the pain.

I walked out to confer with Jackie.

"Any idea how long she's been feeling them?"

"I don't know, Zach, she just called me at work to ask for a ride home. She didn't feel like it would be safe for her to drive."

Not good at all.

As the evening progressed, her pain got worse. I was sitting in my room, just down the hall from my moms' room, and could hear her whimpering. By the time I turned off my light to go to sleep, my mom was sobbing loudly. The medication was incapable of halting her suffering, and there was nothing we could do.

I awoke the next morning to find a note on the kitchen counter, which read:

"Took Mom to the ER, but she's OK, talk soon. xo, Jackie."

My stomach immediately dropped. The last time a family member had been rushed to the ER early in the morning, I'd lost my grandma. I waited anxiously, nearly twitching from stress, until my cell phone finally rang, and I heard Jackie's calm voice on the other end of the line. Mom was safe—still in tremendous pain, but stable. It had been a rough night, to put it mildly.

Terry had been seized by her zingers, unable to talk and jerking violently from all the sensory stimulation of the emergency room—the bright lights and loud doctors amplifying and worsening her deteriorating condition. Worse, the senior doctor on staff refused to listen to Jackie, insisting on an emergency MRI looking for a stroke that Jackie knew wasn't happening.

The law said Jackie was a stranger, and he treated her like one. She was just the woman who had brought the patient in. Jackie knew exactly what was happening and knew exactly what Terry needed. She asked the senior doctor to call the neurologist with whom she had communicated only half an hour earlier and who had the drugs to calm Terry's raging pain. He refused to make the call, and Jackie lacked the legal authority to do anything about it.

To put this in perspective, she says today that the pain she suffered that night was worse—far worse—than the trauma she endured in giving birth to Zebby, an event during which surgeons conducted an emergency C-section without complete anesthesia. That night in the ER, my mom recalls, was the most painful of her life.

I'm not an angry person, and it's not my style to hold a grudge. But if my moms had been married, if Jackie had had the authority she needed, they could have stopped Terry's pain. And they weren't married because—and only because—some people have used the law to inflict their morality on families like mine.

As Terry withered on an ER table deep within the University of Iowa Hospital, once again, in the eyes of the law, the woman by her side was only a stranger.

Some people have pointed out that when I noted in my testimony that "[our] family doesn't derive its sense of worth from being told by the state 'you're married, congratulations!'" it's like saying marriage isn't that big of a deal to us, and if marriage isn't such a big deal, why should the definition of marriage be changed so drastically as to let gay couples get married? If my moms were able to raise my sister and me without being married, then why is the marriage license so important?

It's a valid point, but it also illuminates one of the central issues with the entire same-sex marriage debate. An awful lot of people don't understand that in this country civil marriage entitles the two people who are married to nearly twelve hundred legal rights, privileges, and protections at the federal level and between three hundred to six hundred at the state level, depending on where the couple lives.

Without all of those civil rights, privileges, and protections—and it's worth noting that civil marriage, according to the U.S. Supreme Court on several separate occasions, is in fact a civil right and *not* a privilege—families like mine live in a shadow of second-class citizenship, deprived of privileges as basic as taxation and inheritance rights, partner-survivor benefits, employer-based health insurance, hospital-visitation rights, and the power of medical decision. Over the course of Terry's descent into the wheelchair, our family learned all about those last two.

It's a testament to Jackie's loyalty and commitment that she was willing to ride out the storm knowing full well that our family was not nearly as well protected as families led by married, straight couples.

CHAPTER 11

Clean

For a long time, I kind of viewed Jackie as a stepmom—not because I thought less of her, but because she hadn't been there from the beginning. In my young mind, her departure could come just as easily as her arrival. That's often the way stepparents are viewed. They haven't been there from the beginning, so they might seem like transient figures in the child's life and are often be viewed with a skeptical eye until they prove otherwise. They certainly have to work a little harder to catch up, to earn the love and respect of the child, and prove they are in it for the long haul. My reticence wasn't because Jackie was another woman or because she was gay, it was simply because she was a new member of the family.

To top it off, the new entry to our family was also big on having me make my bed and keep my room neat. (*What is the point of making my bed when I'm just going to get right back in it!*) Terry never really cared much about that sort of thing, but Jackie was always hounding us to have our rooms clean and beds made. She would tell us to clean up our dishes after we finished eating, and when I was a kid, I resented that. Now that I'm living on my own, I'm happy she taught me how to keep a neat house, but I confess I'm a little less diligent about it without her daily reminders. To this day, when I'm at home, Jackie will get on my case if (and when) I forget to bus my dishes or close a cupboard.

And while I'm on the subject of house rules, let me get something off my chest. My mom, ever the health-conscious physician, never let Zebby or me drink soda. Yet Jackie always had a diet Mountain Dew chilling in the refrigerator, and even though it had no sugar, we couldn't drink that, either. Jackie, however, drank it religiously—a double standard that bothered the hell out of me.

When I was in second grade, there was the requisite presentation by the guidance counselor about drugs and smoking. Of course I knew I had never touched, either, but then the counselor mentioned that caffeine was a drug. "It's in soft drinks like Coca-Cola and Mountain Dew," she explained. "And it affects you even more than the sugar."

That got my attention.

I marched home and told Jackie that she shouldn't drink diet Mountain Dew. "Caffeine is a drug!" I said. "It *infects* you." She got very stern and visibly upset with me, and, through clenched teeth, told me to mind my own business. I wasn't old enough for her to discuss with me the value of personal responsibility—how you can choose to do things that might have a negative effect on you as long as it doesn't have a negative effect on others—but that would come soon enough. For now, all I needed to know was that Jackie was in charge as much as my mom was. If she wanted to drink diet Mountain Dew, she could, and I had to keep my mouth shut and my bed made.

I realize now that I had no business telling her what to do, because Jackie was willing to take responsibility for her actions. She had a good health insurance policy, and if drinking lots of soda made her sick or unhealthy, she'd be the one to bear the consequences. Like cleanliness, health is a personal responsibility, and you have to be prepared to deal with the results of your actions.

As I matured I learned more about responsibility and what it means to make decisions. I see parallels between my frustration with what I perceived to be a bad choice on Jackie's part and the anti-LGBT politicians and activists today. But now I see that it doesn't matter if you're drinking diet Mountain Dew or marrying somebody of the same sex—or marrying somebody of the other sex, for that matter. If nobody else is affected—and according to Iowa's largest newspaper, 92 percent of Iowans feel that they haven't been affected by the legalization of same-sex marriage in our state—what's the big deal?

Even if somebody believes that homosexuality is immoral or unclean and that homosexual acts are an affront to God, I have yet to hear how said acts affect anyone other than the people who engage in them. In fact, in the high-profile challenge to California's Proposition 8, the attorney defending California's constitutional ban on same-sex marriage was asked how such unions would harm opposite-sex marriages. After dodging the question numerous times, the attorney was finally called out by the judge and told to answer the question. His response?

"Your Honor, my answer is: I don't know. I don't know."

Terry was the first one to talk to me about sex. She actually got a book that started with, "When a man and a woman love each other very much . . ." Much to my chagrin, the "sex talk" turned out to have serial installments. After high school football practice on one particularly sweltering Iowa afternoon, I found my mom sitting in her van in the parking lot—which was unusual, because our sitter usually picked me up.

I knocked on the window, waking her up from a late-afternoon nap, and climbed into the passenger seat. As always, I started talking nonstop about our agility and strength drills, how my throws were coming along, and then, of course, driving. I was in my final week of driver's ed and thrilled by the prospect of finally finishing. In Iowa, home to one of the country's largest farming populations, driving permits for school are available for students who are fourteen—even to non-farmers' kids. My mom had decided that until I finished driver's ed, I couldn't have passengers in my truck when I drove to and from school (although quite often I would *happen* to see Nic biking to school and would *never* be so rude as to refuse my best friend a ride, rules be damned).

As she drove, my mom listened patiently to my stories. On that afternoon, though, she deviated from the regular route home, pulling into the parking lot of a local coffee shop.

"Aren't we going home?" I asked.

"No," she said. "I think we'll stop for some coffee first."

I was old enough to know that this couldn't be anything good. Puzzled, I got out of the car and helped her into the shop, her leaning on me with an arm and using one of her canes with the other. We staked out a pair of chairs. (I hadn't showered yet, so we were pretty much guaranteed privacy.) She handed me her wallet, and I went and ordered our drinks.

After a few moments, I came back with a cup of tea for me and a mango-coconut smoothie for Mom—her favorite. "No muffins?" she asked, knowing that I've got a soft spot for muffins.

"No," I said. "I thought I'd stick with something healthier."

With an amused look on her face, she said, "Zach, five hours of football in one day. I think a muffin or several would be just fine."

"I don't think you brought me here for a muffin," I said, leaning forward. "So, Mom, what's really on your mind?" I'm running through the list of possibilities in my head. Had Nic's mom seen me driving my truck instead of riding my bike back from work? Had Jackie found the computer games I had hidden in my room?

"Sex," my mom said.

Both relieved and newly tense, I exclaimed, "I knew it!" That was my next thought. Really. "We've been through this before, Mom."

"I know, and it won't be the last," she said.

We had these conversations with annoying regularity, especially now that she knew I was seriously interested in girls. In seventh grade, I had come home raving about this girl, saying that she was the "prettiest, smartest, sweetest . . ." (Never worked out, but she's still seriously pretty.) In eighth grade, when I was caught looking at porn on a computer my mom had brought home from the VA, she had her work techie call me into the hospital to explain why that had been a bad decision. (History and auto-fill are killers.) Luckily her boss was willing to forgive an adolescent male's poor judgment, and she didn't lose her job. After that I talked her into getting me a subscription to *Playboy*. Her only rule? She and Jackie got to look at it first. (They only ever actually enforced that rule once. Jackie's question: "Where's their hair?")

Being a physician-parent, Terry knew she needed to regularly check in with my raging hormones. But as we sat in the coffee shop and sipped our drinks, she said, "I really want to talk about Zebby." I may not have liked baseball, but I knew a curveball when I saw one.

"*What?*" My eyebrows jumped up my forehead and then settled back down at the happy realization that this conversation wasn't about me.

"I read an article in Sunday's paper about teens and sex," she told me. "Apparently girls are starting to be sexually active as early as seventh grade." (Zebby was about to start junior high as a seventh grader.)

"Don't be ridiculous. *Zebby?*"

"Yeah, I know, but—"

"She's not going to do stuff like that, Mom, really. You raised her better than that."

"Okay, but Zebby is going to be asking to go out to do stuff with friends. Maybe she will be asked out for dates at some point. Her estrogen and the boys' testosterone are going to be revving up now that she's in junior high, whether she's ready for it or not." I remember thinking to myself that only a physician would be that technical in a coffee-shop conversation.

I didn't say anything, partly because I knew she was right, but mostly because I'd rather not think about my sister like that.

"The hormones will see to it," she continued. "It's biology. She's going to be out with friends or on a date, and the testosterone parts will want to start groping and fondling the estrogen parts." (You see what I had to deal with?!) "And worse, the estrogen parts might want to start groping for the testosterone parts." She sighed and tossed her head. "But I don't really know when that begins to happen these days. Things are a lot different now than when I was growing up."

"Wait a second, Mom," I said. "How would you know anyway? You weren't going after testosterone parts when you were younger." A keen observation made by the son of a lesbian.

She laughed. "Exactly my point. I don't know how it works, and I need to be careful about Zebby." This was bullshit. "But you know, Zach, once the testosterone gets close enough to the estrogen, your higher brain is often not consulted. Over the millennia, testosterone and estrogen have figured out how to get together."

"I can't believe it," I interrupted, laughing.

"Believe what?"

"You know, sometimes you just amaze me. So strict about TV, computer games, and Xbox, but this is no big deal."

"What?"

"I just think it's funny that it's the lesbian mom who can talk to her son about sex so easily." I tried to imagine Larry sitting Nic down to have a similar conversation. That scene was even funnier than the one I was currently engaged in.

"We still have a couple more things to cover before we can call it a night," she said, interrupting my hilarious thought. "Tell me how your life goes if you, in a moment of passion, become a dad when you're fifteen or sixteen."

"Well, uh," I sputtered. I had *not* been expecting that. "I guess I'd finish high school and go to Kirkwood." Kirkwood was the local community college.

"Who'd support the baby?"

There was a moment of silence as I realized what was going on.

"That was pretty sneaky, Mom, talking about Zebby first."

"Now how would your life turn out if you're not a dad during high school?"

Quietly, I took a moment and looked into my future. I understood her point. The possibility she was describing wasn't pretty. "I don't suppose Grandma talked to you about any of this."

"Grandma did the best she could."

"Yeah? People gave you a hard time growing up?" Now she was on the spot.

"I was alone," she said, nodding and then tapping her temples. "If the world had known what was in my head . . . Well, like I said, it was a different time, so I didn't engage the world much—couldn't let anyone really know who I was, not that *I* was even sure who I was. Not during college, medical school, or even residency. It was during a dark, bleak time in my life that I finally let go of that fear. I became me and allowed myself to live in reality."

I nodded quietly. This was a wrinkle in the conversation I hadn't heard before. I couldn't imagine having to pretend I didn't like girls and couldn't understand why my mom, the kick-ass black belt, would have had to, either.

A few months after I delivered my testimony to the Iowa House Judiciary Committee, I found myself behind the wheel of a fifteen-passenger van on the way to Washington, D.C., with a bunch of friends from the University of Iowa. Riding shotgun was the close friend of one of the trip's organizers. We'd picked her up in Chicago earlier that night. It was now nearly three in the morning and we were somewhere in Ohio.

She had seen the video of the testimony when it initially went viral and was curious to learn more about my family situation. She expressed her strident support for marriage equality, hedging on what I could tell was about to be an awfully uncomfortable question. "So, then," she asked, "what do you think gay people feel? Like, what does homosexuality feel like?"

It wasn't a question I was expecting, and to be honest, was never one that I had considered. Somewhat taken aback, I wondered to myself, what *does* being gay feel like? I had no idea. Though I'd never really thought about what being straight felt like, either. "Well," I said, "I imagine it's probably just like being straight." She cocked her head, waiting for further explanation.

"I guess when I was in junior high," I admitted, "I started getting these feelings that I'd never had before about these girls in my classes. I didn't really know what they were. I just knew that they felt good and made me a little anxious, and they made these girls super interesting. And then I started to get erections at the most awkward times."

She laughed and nodded.

I'd always known that girls had noticed.

"So, then, you grow up a bit and you either realize independently or are told that these feelings are sexual feelings, and basically, that that's what it means to be straight. To have these feelings, I mean, about people of the other sex. I'm guessing that basically gay people feel the exact same thing, but about people of the same sex."

She nodded.

"You know," I continued, "they probably just start having these feelings, these thoughts about people, but they are about people of the same sex. It's not like I woke up one morning, cracked my knuckles and thought, *All right, time to pick a sexuality. I pick straight*, or something. It was sort of this realization that I liked girls and was sexually attracted to them and then figured out, oh, well then that means I'm straight. For gay people it's probably pretty much the same thing, but then the realization is different. There's probably some shame in there, maybe, because we still live in a pretty homophobic society . . ."

I trailed off, my thoughts going back to all the times in junior high and high school I encountered the casual discrimination and homophobia that seemed, at times, omnipresent.

"Yeah," she said, sounding satisfied. "I guess I hadn't thought about it like that. Yeah, that makes a lot of sense. Nice."

I hadn't ever thought about it like that, either, but it did make an awful lot of sense.

THE MERITS OF CLEANLINESS

"A Scout keeps his body and mind fit and clean." Some days I don't shower. I just lounge around and browse the Internet or play video games—these are fun days. My hair gets greasy, my roommates give me the occasional side-eye, and I feel kind of gross. But, of course, I would never walk into a business meeting in such a state, and when I finally do clean up, I feel great. A large part of cleanliness is knowing what is and isn't appropriate.

You have to decide for yourself what clean is, but you also have to recognize that if other people don't fit your standards of clean but they aren't hurting anyone else, then there is no valid reason for discrimination against them. Whether or not a person has mud on his or her face is pretty immaterial to who that person actually is. Whether someone keeps a clean house doesn't affect me. As I mentioned in the introduction, when people talk negatively about my having two moms, I often feel as though I'm being told I'm wearing different-colored socks. They might find it unsightly, but if it doesn't harm them, what's the big deal? When a person's actions don't affect anyone else, when the consequences of those actions don't breach another person's consent, I have a difficult time believing that that action can be deemed "immoral" or "unclean" in a logical or rational fashion.

This applies to sexuality as well. Am I attracted to men or aroused by the thought of sleeping with a guy? Not at all. That being said, I do have other sexual interests and kinks that you might not find particularly engaging, just as there are plenty of other possibilities that I don't find interesting. But unless what you're doing in your sex life directly affects me or hurts other people, I really don't care and I certainly wouldn't have the gall to try to change what you're doing so long as both (or all, if that's your thing) parties involved are involved of their own volition.

Consent is, in my mind, the ultimate test for morality. There's nothing immoral about drinking diet soda or purchasing a *Playboy* subscription because neither one negatively affects anyone else's rights to life, liberty, or the pursuit of happiness. Just because something isn't healthy or not to your taste doesn't necessarily mean it's immoral. I can smoke a cigarette alone—something that is decidedly unhealthy—without it being immoral because it's *my* life and *my* liberty, but put me in a room smoking around a bunch of toddlers and I'd have some serious moral questions about secondhand smoke.

Crimes like rape, murder, and theft are all decidedly immoral because they violate the victim's right to live as he or she chooses. They take place without the victim's consent, depriving that person of his or her power to choose. You can also give consent but not enjoy it. We all consent to pay our taxes, but I don't know anybody who looks forward to filing them or wants to hug an IRS agent. (Although at the time of this writing, Congress is less popular than the IRS, which says something about Congress.) We are all people with inherent worth and dignity, and when you violate a person's right to consent, you reduce them to less than a person—rendering them merely an object lacking both agency and the power of choice.

One afternoon on a camping outing with my family when I was about eight years old, I found that we needed some more firewood. With Jackie in tow, we wandered around our campground, seeing if there might be some fellow campers who had some spare logs. Not far down the road was an older family enjoying the beautiful fall afternoon. The patriarch was smoking.

In the second-grade lesson where my classmates and I learned about drugs like caffeine, we had also been informed—in vigorous terms—of the dangers of smoking. Smoking was bad. This was a message that my we-both-work-in-medicine moms had reinforced at home. Never stated, but naturally inferred, was that if smoking was bad, people who smoked were bad. Right?

Here I was faced with a real, live smoker, so I did what you might expect any second grader in my shoes to do: I freaked out. Jackie had no idea what was going on or why I was so uncomfortable, but I practically dragged her back to our campsite without taking the extra firewood the family was happily offering.

Concerned about why I was so upset, Jackie asked what was wrong.

"He was *smoking*," I said. "Didn't you see? He's a bad man."

Jackie gave me a blank look and almost burst out laughing.

It was a difficult concept for me to wrap my eight-year-old mind around, but there's a difference between unhealthy and bad, just like there's a difference between unclean and immoral. It might be unhealthy to smoke or unclean to not shower, but as long as your secondhand smoke isn't being inhaled by someone who doesn't want to inhale it and your stench isn't knocking anyone out, neither one is bad or immoral, per se.

To dig into this point a bit, there's nothing inherently immoral about eating pork, but if you're an observant Muslim, it's an affront to God. Orthodox Jews maintain similar dietary restrictions and violating those is also deemed immoral. But it's important to understand that such violations of religious dogma are only unethical because the religion says so. Personally I certainly don't find the consumption of shrimp to be immoral. It's actually one of my favorite foods. But I'm not going to inflict my views of what is or isn't moral food on anyone else.

And it's more than just food.

To many conservative Christians, sleeping with somebody of the same sex means that you have committed a sin. In some denominations, working on the Sabbath is considered immoral. Tattoos are thought by many to be unclean due to religious beliefs. But tattoos are increasingly popular, Walmart is open twenty-four hours, and the U.S. Supreme Court has ruled that so-called antisodomy laws are unconstitutional and a violation of personal privacy rights.

There are countries in the world where religious beliefs and dogma are codified into law. Iran, Saudi Arabia, Pakistan, and plenty of other countries are legitimate theocracies. The United States of America is not one of those countries. To believe that *your* path to God is the *only* path to God and to go out of your way to prevent others from walking their own paths and living their own lives is not just heartless, but in a very real way, it is un-American.

It is a travesty that two opposite-gendered atheists (and I use this as a meaningful descriptor, not a pejorative) can fly to Las Vegas and be married by an Elvis impersonator, but a marine coming home from back-to-back-to-back-to-back tours in Afghanistan and Iraq cannot marry the man he loves. And that's not to slam atheists at all but to simply observe that this debate is so bogged down by homophobia that two people for whom religion is meaningless can still get married *if* they are of opposite genders, but reverent people of the same gender cannot. Some people are incapable of seeing that that sentiment, as well-intentioned as those people who believe in it may be, is a destructive force fueled by arrogance that has no place in the laws of this country. We may seem to be stuck at a moral crossroads, but if you don't get upset if my moms get married, I won't get upset that your religion suggests homosexuality is a sin. This arrangement may not be perfect, but this is how democracies are—messy.

The last thing I'll say about cleanliness is this: People obviously have different standards of what is and isn't clean, what is and isn't moral. You can choose to only spend your time with the people who agree with you, but don't try to enforce your standards of cleanliness or morality on others. I once heard that you are a reflection of the six people you spend the most time with. If those six people are cool with who you are, that's awesome, more power to you. But let's make a deal—you can choose the people you want to spend your time with, and I can choose mine.

CHAPTER 12

Thrifty

When we first moved to Iowa City, I was still using a heel lift to compensate for the slightly stunted growth of my left leg, a by-product of an incident in day care that left me with a fractured femur. It wasn't a major inconvenience, but I was still lagging behind my peers in athletic ability. I had been doing my morning hops as physical therapy for years, but my moms knew they needed something else to accelerate my recovery.

So Jackie came up with a plan. If I ran on the treadmill for thirty minutes three times a week for six months, she would buy me an acoustic guitar. She worked with me to get me up to speed, starting at a brisk walking pace and gradually building up to a steady jog. If I'd tried to jump in to a fast jog, I don't think I would have gotten very far. Even with our gradual progression, adhering to the plan wasn't easy. But I stuck to it, often cueing up my favorite TV shows or movies in our basement to watch while I ran.

Slowly but surely I began to catch up to my peers, and by the time the six months were over at the end of my fourth-grade year, I had stopped wearing the heel lift—and I had an acoustic guitar. Great success. However, like a lot of guys my age, I wound up realizing that I liked the idea of the guitar more than the guitar itself. Today, before I make a major purchase, I figure out if I actually want what I'm buying or if I just like the idea of owning it.

As hokey as it might sound, the biggest gift of Jackie's exercise plan wasn't the guitar but the lessons I learned along the way. By having a plan and an end goal, I had a grasp on what I wanted, how I would achieve it, and what success would mean. Having such a clear plan made sticking to it much easier. Without that clarity, both of the plan and of the goal, it would have been easy to think, *Oh, yeah, well, I can just skip a jog this week*. But with such well-defined terms, I learned about honesty. Sometimes Jackie had to take my word that I did the thirty minutes of jogging before she got home. I knew that I could have gotten away with lying, but if I had done so, it would have tarnished the results. Yeah, I wanted the guitar, but I wanted to get back on equal footing even more, and I couldn't lie my way to that.

Like I said, the guitar wound up gathering dust in the basement, but the values and maxims I learned in my pursuit of it have stuck with me ever since.

Jackie's always been good at giving gifts, both abstract and tangible. Some people might call the process of remembering when gifts should be given, buying them, and wrapping them as a "wife thing," or think of that as stereotypically feminine, but doesn't that sound . . . old-fashioned? When you think about it—or at least when I think about it—gift giving and thoughtfulness seem pretty asexual, just like perseverance and honesty. But maybe that's because my other mom was never good at gift giving, in the "presents" sense of the word, so to claim that *all* women are good at gift giving, or should be good at gift giving, is silly. In fact, if it wasn't for Jackie, my sister and I would probably have gotten Math Blaster computer games every Christmas or nothing at all.

I remember that one of Jackie and Terry's early disagreements was over gift giving. Terry had to sit down with Jackie and explain to her that if Jackie wanted a gift for a particular occasion, Terry needed her to make a "list for Santa" that had exactly what she wanted on it and write reminders of the event on a big wall calendar in the kitchen. Jackie said that if Terry really loved her, she would know what Jackie would want for a gift, but as Terry put it, she just "isn't wired that way." She has no skill whatsoever at picking up on those subtle social signals, no matter how many times Jackie hint-hints about what she likes. Even though Terry was—and still is—a brilliant medical doctor and down-to-earth woman, that kind of stuff was always a little over her head.

So even though there may be a cultural expectation that all women are great at finding gifts for their family members and friends, I learned at a pretty young age that that wasn't actually the case. Furthermore, it became clear to me very early on that a person's sex didn't actually tell me much about that person at all.

The reality is that not only is my mom unimpressive at gift selection but she also finds the whole ordeal of exchanging presents rather uncomfortable. She has never sought validation in the latest gadget or gizmo and has never cared greatly for material possessions. While a lot of people thought it was important to keep up with the Joneses, she never has and doesn't find gratification in giving someone something they really didn't need. But Terry knows the power of gift giving and that the right gift at the right time can be tremendously powerful, and understands that the sentiment is what really matters.

With her first paycheck as a medical intern, she bought her mom a washer and dryer because her mother had been doing her laundry by hand for decades. Grandma Lois, a stoic member of the Silent Generation, got misty and her lips quivered as she thanked Terry for the gift and warned her that there was no way her husband, John, would allow it. Sure enough, Grandpa John insisted on paying for the washer and dryer in full and told Terry to spend the money elsewhere. So, ever the rebel (or thoughtful daughter, depending on your vantage point), Terry set up a monthly fifty-dollar allowance for her mother, so that she might have some financial independence and could spend a little money without having to ask her husband's permission.

For Grandma Lois, the gift wasn't really the washer and dryer or even the allowance. It was the satisfaction of knowing her daughter had not only excelled in college but also had gone on to medical school and was now employed as a physician. Grandma Lois had never made it past high school and here was her daughter-turned-doctor moving up in the world. But even as Terry moved forward, she remembered whence she came. When Terry told me this story, I asked how she had known to get Grandma Lois such a good gift. She pointed out that there's a world of difference between being incapable of picking up on hints and seeing an obvious need, like when your mother is doing the backbreaking work of manually washing laundry. I thought this was a fair point.

When it came to gifts for my moms, they always insisted that my sister and I could not just buy something from the store. They preferred that we *make* them something instead. (Which is how my short-lived rap career was born—and died. But seriously, A&R, get at me.) This wasn't about saving money. They wanted a part of us—that's what really meant something to them—something they could cherish. Our house is now a museum of things that Zebby and I crafted as presents for birthdays, holidays, and special occasions. Zebby and I weren't always thrilled with this arrangement, and we certainly didn't want them to make things for us. Like most kids, we still wanted toys. Fortunately we had Jackie there for that.

Our house, though, was certainly thrifty. We recycled, we turned off the lights when we left the room, and my moms bought much of our food in bulk. When I was in kindergarten, one of the early years with the *Teaching Your Kids Values* book, we instituted a family bank. The authors suggested "a large wooden box with a lock and a slot in the top for deposits." Terry decided to recycle a used Skippy peanut butter jar. And why spend money on a lock? We had already learned trust. The plastic screw-on cap, accessible to all, would suffice.

The idea behind the family bank was to teach frugality and discipline (read: thriftiness) and, most important, to teach those things in a fun, engaging way. On Sundays we'd get our allowances and we'd make contributions to the family bank. They'd be used for trips to our favorite water park, Rainbow Falls, which was about half an hour away and made for a great way to spend an afternoon.

When I was a few years older, my mom started a savings account at the local branch of Associated Bank, a major financial institution in central Wisconsin. The cool part was that Associated Bank worked with my elementary school to let kids make deposits. Every Friday a bank rep would come over and work with sixth graders to set up an ad hoc teller line in the school library, and my third-grade class would walk over every Friday so those of us with accounts could make deposits.

After moving to Iowa, I learned how to open my own checking account, write checks, and budget my money. Plus I found out about investments and that sort of thing. It was Grandpa John who had impressed upon my mom the value of knowing how to keep track of money. Fresh out of high school, he had started a trucking business, but he hadn't been responsible in managing it. He took only the jobs that were convenient, passing on those that weren't and missing valuable opportunities to grow his business. Soon he lost his truck. Almost immediately afterward, he was drafted to fight in World War II.

Upon his return from the Pacific, with the disciplined lessons of the military instilled in his mind, he started trucking again and never turned down a job. Before long he had six trucks and a small staff working for him, but his father told him that he couldn't raise a family like that and encouraged him to take up farming—a more suitable profession for an Iowa family man. So he left his trucking business, purchased some land on Highway 76, and continued the family tradition while creating a new one: saving and investing while living far beneath his means.

Yes, Terry learned that value from her father, but she didn't need to be a man to pass her father's wisdom on to me.

I was two days away from heading off to my first Boy Scouts camp, and it was time to pack. Mom and I were standing out on our three-season porch, an array of clothes, camping gear, food, and Scouting paraphernalia sprawled across the wooden floor, all surrounding a well-worn, in places frayed, authentic backpacker's backpack that was at least twice as old as me. I was struggling to see how a week's worth of supplies would all fit.

"If you roll your socks and underwear up, instead of just tossing them in there, you can cut down on a lot of wasted space," my mom said, pointing to one of the side pockets. "You know, when I went to Nepal, I had three *months'* worth of gear in this thing."

Inside, Jackie was at the dinner table, reviewing my medical paperwork—a history of asthma, a spiral fracture in my left femur at age three that had required surgery and still occasionally gave me trouble, seasonal allergies that would probably flare up—and double-checking my merit badge requirements.

Zebby was sulking. "Girl Scouts never get to do anything fun," she protested.

Even as I worked through the backpack puzzle, I was excited. This was my first year as an actual Boy Scout, and after seven years in the Cub Scouts, I was ready for the adventures Camp Wakonda promised and the lessons I'd learn in my merit badge workshops. And I knew I'd get there with the support of my mom's backpack.

At the beginning of each year, she and I sat down and budgeted all my expenses for the coming twelve months. She would give me a monthly allowance that would cover most of my expenses but reminded me that I had to work for leisure money and that my family chores didn't qualify as "work." As a result, my mom was always encouraging me to be entrepreneurial, which is one of the reasons I was so interested in business from such a young age.

So it probably makes sense that Entrepreneurship became one of my favorite Scout merit badges. While it isn't Eagle required, I think it should be. Successful entrepreneurs are usually good leaders, which is a trait that the BSA values and pretty much defines what it means to be an Eagle Scout.

I've always had the entrepreneurial spirit, always wanted to work for myself and have that independence. And my mom, the physician, made it very clear to me, and she's reminded me ever since, that if I wanted money, I had to work for it. It didn't just happen or grow on trees. It was a choice. My first business venture wasn't a lemonade stand, though; it was offering gardening services at three dollars an hour. My pitch was simple: I would weed your garden at an incredibly good price. I had a flier and a logo and everything. While not wildly successful, I did pull some weeds and make a little green.

In our weekly Entrepreneurship merit badge sessions, I learned how to start a business, not necessarily the right way but effectively. Our instructor emphasized this point, saying, "There is not a right way or wrong way." You had to do what worked, and if what you were doing didn't work, he told us to do something different.

I've since learned that ideas are a dime a dozen; execution is everything. (Hence, the infamous line from one of my generation's defining films, *The Social Network*, "If you were the inventors of Facebook, you would have invented Facebook.") I learned the lessons that shaped my life from my family's nightly conversations about values, and in Scouting I got to put those values into practice, weaving into my moral fiber what it means to be a good person. My mothers have watched, and led, with strong support.

I remember the first big paycheck I got was for two hundred dollars for edging our neighbor's lawn. Nic and I shared the work and the pay and were super excited. I still have a photocopy of that check somewhere in my moms' basement. After finishing the Entrepreneurship merit badge, Nic and I teamed up again to start J & W Home Care. It was "Home Care" because we didn't just do lawns, we were willing to wash your clothes or watch your kids—whatever the clients wanted, within reason.

Budgeting is important for any successful endeavor, and it was a family value that Terry applied to everything—including my long, hot showers.

When I'd get home from swimming practice, I'd usually take a superlong shower, ostensibly because I wanted to make sure I got all of the chlorine off my skin. Mom said, "Fine. . . . But if you're going to do this, you'll have to pay for it." So if the water bill for a month was over sixty dollars, Zebby and I had to pay not just the difference, but split the entire balance. And after one month of a few too many long showers, sure enough, my mom withdrew thirty-five dollars from my checking account. After that, I developed a sense of self-discipline pretty quickly.

Later I got my first vehicle, a used pickup truck that was as old as I was and cost three thousand dollars. The truck ran pretty well, but I hadn't anticipated gas in my budget for that year. I went to my mom and told her, "Gas is expensive."

"I know," she said. "You'll have to figure that out. Sometimes we don't budget enough and have to make tough decisions."

It really wasn't that tough of a decision. I mowed a few more lawns, because I knew what I wanted and was willing to work to get it.

THE MERITS OF THRIFTINESS

In Scouts, thrift isn't just another tenet of the law. Thrift moves beyond just monetary aspects because of our adherence to the outdoor philosophy known as "pack it in, pack it out." When we'd go out camping, we couldn't be burdened down by excess equipment or food. We took what we needed—no more, no less. *"A Scout works to pay his own way and to help oth-*

ers. He saves for unseen needs. He protects and conserves natural resources. He carefully uses time and property."

When I went to Boy Scout camp, I used the backpack my mom used when she went to Nepal and Tibet, where she witnessed firsthand how little one needs to survive. The backpack is from the early 1980s but still works fine. I used to love packing it, knowing I only had so much room and had to decide what was absolutely essential. I always tried to save room for a *Star Wars* book.

Before each camping adventure, one Scout is put in charge of organizing meals for the weekend. It's a requirement you have to meet before you can achieve the First Class rank. Feeding an entire troop entails the careful planning of a number of meals, making a budget, going grocery shopping, transporting the food safely, making the meals, serving the meals, and, of course, cleaning up afterward. Everything we *didn't* use also had to be removed from the campsite, part of the "pack it in, pack it out" philosophy. I discovered that while it takes a little work upfront to be thrifty, you wind up saving a lot of energy in the long run.

When it was my turn to organize the meals, Jackie and I sat down and carefully planned out the meals we wanted to make. There were a bunch of meal suggestions in the standard-issue *Boy Scout Handbook*, so we drew most of our ideas from there. But I remember what I made for breakfast most clearly: pancakes.

Pancakes were my favorite. For Mother's Day (which is, as you might imagine, kind of a big deal for my family), my sister and I would almost always make our moms breakfast in bed. And by "my sister and I," I mean mostly "me." Though I wasn't the best cook, I definitely enjoyed the ritual of preparing breakfast. Experimenting with different pancake flavors and ingredient combinations was practically a part-time hobby for me. Chocolate-chip pancakes, strawberry pancakes, apple-and-cinnamon pancakes, the options go on and on—and let's not even get into the syrup choices.

With Boy Scouts, though, gourmet pancakes were off the table, or at least off the griddle, due to budgetary concerns. I decided to go with small, plain pancakes and scrambled eggs with ham and cheese. I'd also bring apple cider packets so we could have something warm to drink on the cold winter morning.

At the grocery store I quickly realized that if I were going to have my prized Aunt Jemima syrup, I'd have to go with the less expensive store brand for the pancake mix. It worked out though, because the store-brand mix came in a box that didn't have as much packaging, making my job of cleaning up a whole lot easier.

I had come in under budget. Jackie helped me keep track of the receipt—I was notoriously bad at holding on to my wallet at that age—so I could be reimbursed by the troop. My fellow Scouts considered the meals rousing successes, and I agreed, even though I had to get up at six in the morning to start cooking.

I had wanted the name brand for both my syrup and my mix, but it simply wasn't in my budget, so I made do with what I had. It might sound simple, but it's a principle that I think America has gotten away from over the last few decades. We've forgone a habit of savings (that's *so* 1950s) and become a culture of credit. According to the U.S. Department of Commerce, the average American savings rate peaked in 1982 at around 9 percent of annual income. In 2008, immediately before the beginning of the Great Recession, the average American savings rate was around 5.5 percent. That's a 60 percent decrease in less than thirty years.

Why? We're spending above our means to keep up with the Joneses. They have a pool. We want one. They have an iPhone. We want one. They drive a Mercedes. We want one. We want distractions. We want luxury. We want, we want, we want. And rather than earn it, we use credit to quench our thirst for the material and extend ourselves far beyond our means.

To live in a society defined by consumption, we pay the highest costs. Our fascination with the things we own becomes an addiction. Slipping test scores, strict adherence to pop culture, incessantly comparing ourselves to others—these aren't diseases; they're symptoms of a lifestyle obsession. (A "lifestyle choice," maybe?) As time passes, the objects we once used to define ourselves no longer belong to us, and the final question we are left with is not, "Who owns what?" but rather, "What owns who?"

Fortunately I had two parents that taught me that if I want something I have to work for it and, beyond survival, there are only a few things with inherent value: love, family, community, and doing unto others as you would have them do unto you. It was an uphill battle at times—the culture of consumption pervades pop culture and we are exposed to nearly one thousand advertisements per day—but our nightly values conversations proved to be an effective remedy against the culture of want.

But sometimes, as we'd occasionally discuss over dinner, work wasn't enough. Sometimes there are things that are beyond our control—the privilege of being born in America, for instance, or having loving parents—that can shape our lives for the better. Other times, like with an MS diagnosis, they can set us back and we have to just roll with the punches. In order to effectively play your hand, you have to know the value of your cards—you can't just take them for granted—a lesson my moms taught me early and often.

My mom and I were deep in the network of subterranean passages and beautiful hollows that make up Maqouketa (Mah-KOH-keh-tah) Caves, a state park about two hours north of Iowa City. We reclined on the granite floor, and I set my hardhat next to us, providing just enough light to make out the cavern's stunning formations. I was eleven years old at the time and hadn't yet learned about her MS diagnosis. All I knew was that she needed help getting around and had told me that I'd have to carry our water and food and we'd need to take frequent breaks—but if that was all I had to do, I was on board.

As Terry recharged during our latest rest phase, she shared stories from the last time she'd gone backpacking. She'd been in the Himalayan mountains (now *there's* an adventure) as part of the Direct Relief International program. Upon her graduation from medical school and the completion of her residency, she'd decided to spend a year volunteering and putting her newly acquired skills to good use. She spent time in the Caribbean, Nepal, and Tibet, working in impoverished communities that badly needed her medical expertise. The Caribbean had been bad, but Nepal and Tibet were destitute.

It was in the mountains of the Himalayas that she had acquired her distaste for material excess. How, she wondered, could so many people use and waste so much when so many others went without even the most basic necessities? In that cave, she explained to me that in Tibet there were no beds and no running water.

"You mean they have to drink water like in this cave?" I said, excited about the possibility of being able to camp out here actually *in* a cave.

"That's right, but it's not safe, Zach. They only do that because they have no other choice, not because they want to."

"Oh . . ."

"In fact, they don't even have toilet paper."

"*What?*"

"That's right. They have to use their left hand to wipe. That's why they only eat with their right hands in Tibet." She'd occasionally made South Asian food, and whenever she did, she'd encouraged us to try eating only with our right hand. Never one to shy away from *not* using utensils, I jumped at the chance, although now that I understood why, I thought it was kind of gross.

"Eww," I laughed.

"Never forget how lucky we are, Zach. I know sometimes things might seem tough, especially my needing to rest all the time now, but we are incredibly, incredibly blessed to have what we have. Never forget that."

What I see now is that the struggle of my family is the struggle of every American family: to find love, strength, and meaning in a world that is often uncooperative, occasionally hostile, and, at times, even dangerous. Our challenge is to make the best of the hand we've been dealt without forgetting why we're playing the game in the first place. Success—be it monetary, academic, or professional—is of little value when the most fundamental parts of our identity have been obscured or lost in the pursuit of that success.

Back in the cave, I nodded.

I'd never thought of toilet paper as a luxury before, but boy was she right.

To me, thrifty is a combination of knowing what's actually valuable and recognizing the work it takes to earn it. I'm not opposed to nice things. In fact I own a number of gaming systems, a high-def TV, nice clothes, some stupidly expensive cologne, and plenty of toilet paper. But I worked my ass off so I could pay with cash, and I use all of them frequently. What I'm against is conspicuous consumption. There is too much need in the world to spend all our time chasing decadent, superfluous wants when we can't even afford them in the first place.

We are better than that.

CHAPTER 13

Brave

By the time I walked through the doors of Iowa City West High, I had already mastered my standard answer to kids who asked questions about what my mom and dad did. I could say, "Oh, they both work in health care," without so much as a blink.

I knew by then that my family life was not what society considered normal.

It was finally in science class that I stumbled. It was a fortunate hesitation in that it finally released me from my constant apprehension and fear, and gave me the courage to live my own truth.

I was sitting at a two-person desk, working with my partner on our lab exercises. Ms. Secrist, our teacher, was walking around the room checking our progress and casually chatting with her students. She was a tall, attractive woman in her early thirties, the kind of teacher kids think of as pretty. "So,

Zach," she said, suddenly stopping by my chair. "What do your parents do?"

"Well," I stammered, trying to focus on the task at hand. "Um. My mom's a doctor and my other mo . . ." and then I trailed off. I looked up at her. She had caught me off guard. I took a moment, glanced at my lab partner, recovered, and issued my standard line: "They're both in the medical profession."

She smiled, nodded, and moved on to the next table.

Shit.

For the rest of class, I couldn't focus on what we were doing. Though I stayed calm on the surface, internally I was freaking out. Science was the last class of the day, so after the bell rang, I made a beeline for the door and was almost there before I heard, "Hey, Zach, could you hang on a minute?"

Nope. Can't. Have to go to football practice. "Umm . . . sure." *No! What?! Football. Go!*

After the rest of my classmates left the room—including Nic, who had given me a you're-screwed kind of look on his way out the door—Ms. Secrist came over to me. "Zach," she said, looking at me with smiling eyes. "Don't worry. I saw you hesitated there when I asked you what your parents did. I want you to know it's cool. This is a safe place. You're safe here."

I nodded and scurried off to football. I tried to figure out what had just happened as I strapped on my pads. I found it difficult to stay on point when I took snaps on the field. It wasn't a good practice, and my teammates noticed.

During a water break I talked with Jake, a buddy of mine who played strong tackle. I'd been playing ball with him since seventh grade. He had met my moms and, despite having more conservative parents, was totally fine with who my parents were.

"Hey, Jake," I said, as we were putting our helmets back on. "You can't like . . . *tell* that I've got two moms, right? Like, you can't just look at me and figure it out?"

Jake gave me this kind of puzzled look and then just laughed. "You're kidding . . . right?"

When I got home that night, I didn't say anything to my moms about what Ms. Secrist had said. There really wasn't much to say. I hadn't yet realized that her steadying words would set me on the journey that culminated in the writing of this book. But looking back, without Ms. Secrist's affirmation that her classroom was a safe place, without her kind words and calming smile, I never would have had the courage to do what I did next: come out, for my parents, to my high school.

Freshmen don't actually get to write for the school's newspaper, *West Side Story.* You spend that first year taking Journalism Lab, learning how to structure a story (inverted pyramid, anyone?), figuring out how to conduct a successful interview, and learning the differences between hard news and opinion writing, among other things. Even though I enjoyed writing hard-news stories, and especially sports-related articles, I particularly enjoyed writing opinion pieces. In my journalism class, I discovered that I have a distinct voice and that the limitations of hard-news writing cramped my style. (I once got in trouble for writing in the news section that Marcus Theatres, a local movie theatre chain, had no comment on their plans to take over the world. Which, technically, was true but, evidently, was also inappropriate. Worse, it cost me an A in that class.)

Our teacher and the newspaper's official advisor, Ms. Schlesinger (or, as we called her, "The Schless") was generally pretty nice but also very strict—corralling a bunch of high schoolers into producing a newspaper requires a healthy amount of discipline. She also had a keen eye for recognizing words with social merit or when someone exposed a painful truth.

During the second trimester of the year, late winter, we were given our first column assignment. Sitting at the computer in my moms' living room, finally given the opportunity to write about *anything* my heart desired, my mind kept coming back to the first thing I had heard when I walked through the doors of West High on my first day of school: "Hey, fag! Get over here." It hadn't been directed at me, or at anyone I knew, but made immediately clear, on day one, that it was going to be a long four years.

After I turned in my piece, I quickly forgot about it, because I was more concerned with the rapidly approaching district-wide swim tournament and my growing appreciation for rap. I'd been a hard-rock kind of guy through most of junior high, but there were always a couple of rap albums on my iPod mini. (*So gangsta.*) Now I was starting to listen to Eminem, 50 Cent, Young Jeezy, and Game, fueled in part by Michael Phelps's admission that he listened to Young Jeezy's "Go Getta" before every race. I had to bleach my hair (a swimming tradition followed by high school teams everywhere) and then shave my head—and the rest of my body—in preparation for the biggest races of the year. Competition would be tight and every second, and hair, counted.

I was so focused on the upcoming swim meet that I forgot all about the column. But Ms. Schlesinger got it back to me quickly, and to my initial dismay, it was covered in red ink. Clearly she hadn't liked it. "Zach," the Schless began, with a serious look on her face. *Damn. I thought it was pretty good.* "I think you should run this in the paper this month."

I did a double take. Not what I was expecting.

"You . . . you, what?"

"I think it's really, really good, and Miriam does, too." Miriam was the paper's columns editor.

I looked again at the column and realized Miriam had been the one to mark it up; she'd edited it for publication. Below my final sentence she had written and underlined, "This is really, really good. Let's run it!"

I wasn't nearly as enthusiastic, and told the Shless I had to think it over.

Sixteen days later, after a rigorous internal debate, the *West Side Story* ran my very first column:

> *"Look at that loser, what a fag," "Check it out! See Katy? That's soo gay!" "What do you want queer?" These are phrases that everybody hears every day. Some people may be numb to it, but every single time I hear one of these derogatory epithets, I flinch and typically tell the person to cut it out. These insults affect me personally. Why? I have lesbian parents. The first words I heard when I walked into West High on August 22 were, "Hey fag! Get over here!" I was disgusted.*
>
> *This year an estimated 276,000 American high*

school students will try to kill themselves. Only
5,000 will succeed. Of that 5,000, 650 will identify
as homosexual, making LGBT students nearly three
times as likely as their straight peers to take their
own life. Maybe this isn't surprising when you consider that LGBT youth are twice as likely to be
threatened or injured by a weapon at school than
their heterosexual peers are. This makes "coming
out" a very dangerous process. It's particularly hard
for people who are surrounded by extremely conservative people.

Why is there such a negative attitude towards homosexuals? Actually, I think the answer is rather
simple. People fear what they don't understand. To
hide their fear, they act as though they're afraid of it
all the time. I can't be sure though, because I have
never had a negative attitude towards homosexuals.
That's what I get for living with two lesbians, I guess.
We live in Iowa City, and I like to think of Iowa City
as a very diverse and accepting community. Most of
the time when people hear that I have lesbian parents, the conversation normally goes along these
lines:

"You have lesbian parents?"

"Yep."

"Cool. Are they hot?"

I laugh. "No."

Most of the time that's the entire conversation.
I've lost a few friends from that, but not too many.
The part of this that frustrates me the most is that

most people who use those terms in a derogatory way really haven't gotten to know a gay or lesbian person. Yet, they still use the term in a demeaning way. Seriously, if you're going to discriminate against somebody, at least talk to them for a little while first. That's just being polite.

Lots of LGBT youth are accepted by their friends and family. Unfortunately, many, many are not. I think that part of the reason that they are not always accepted is the environment that is unintentionally created by our use of these words. When the term is used in a demeaning way, it can seem that being gay automatically means you're a loser. That's obviously not true. I know quite a few "non-straight" individuals. You might be surprised how "regular" they are.

So, do me a favor. The next time you hear somebody say, "Look at that fag," or "What a queer," ask them to think about what they just said. Maybe someday we'll attend a school where you are defined by your character and not by your sexual orientation. But, without a lot of self-restraint, I sincerely doubt it.

A guy can dream.

The *West Side Story* always comes out on a Friday. District championships had taken place already. Since I was no longer driving to school at six in the morning for swim practice, I got to "sleep in" until seven thirty. I pulled in to my school's parking lot well aware that it was publication day. I wasn't really sure what to expect. I walked up to the building and there were two *WSS* staff members handing out copies of the paper. I always enjoyed reading it—and had to for my journalism class—so I took one, busying myself in the articles.

As I walked to my first-period class, I bumped into a few friends who had already read the column and thought it was spot-on. That was good to hear. Maybe it was because I was pretty tall for my grade, or maybe because I had a buzz cut that made me look older than I was, or maybe it was just the fact that it wasn't a big deal, but I didn't get a single piece of negative feedback that morning, or the rest of the day—or at all.

I kept hearing those offensive words and kept asking people to cut it out, but I also found people catching themselves starting to use the word "fag" or "gay" and then, midsentence, opting for a different phrasing.

Really the biggest reaction happened after I got home. I left my copy on the kitchen counter because Jackie liked to read the paper, too, and her subscription wouldn't arrive for a few days.

I was back in my room, working through my geometry homework, when I got called to the kitchen for supper. Jackie still had tears in her eyes, and Terry was positively beaming, a rare occurrence those days. They hugged me without saying a word.

Nothing needed to be said.

One cool morning in the late spring of my junior year, Zebby walked into the garage and saw Terry lowering the seat on my bike. (Well, technically, it was her bike, but I'd been using it for the last two years.) Zebby instantly knew what Mom was up to—the helmet she was wearing was another giveaway. Zebby, distressed, opened the door to the house and shouted out for Jackie and me.

I was in the kitchen, reading the paper, and quickly ran into the garage. As soon as I saw what Mom was going to attempt, I immediately tried to talk her out of it. It had been nearly a decade since she had ridden her bike. But following the e-stim, her recovery was picking up steam. She was still a long, long way from being fully healthy, but it was impossible to deny that she was getting better. This, however, seemed like an unnecessary risk, and one I did not want her to take—a sentiment I expressed forcefully.

She had been falling less, but having already watched her strength fail her many times before, I didn't want her to jeopardize what seemed to be an extraordinarily fragile recovery. I knew if she went down in a bad way, there was going to be a lot of pain and suffering, but not just for her, for all of us. I did not fully understand *why* she was getting better, and without that understanding, I did not understand the state she was in. Not only had her strength been returning, but her stamina and balance had been as well. She was confident that she could do this.

Jackie was also skeptical but more trusting in Terry's judgment than I was. Looking back, I can see why. Terry, after all, had been the first to recognize that her body was failing her. However she had also always been stubborn. Once she set her mind to something and that look of steely determination came into her eyes, you knew better than to go against her will.

"Jackie," my mom said, as she clutched the bike. "If you don't think I should, I won't."

Looking for a way to get a handle on the situation, I suggested that if she was really going to do this, then Zebby and I would jog alongside her and Jackie would ride behind her.

Earlier that summer Jackie and I had enjoyed an amazing biking trip to Utah, one that was both exhilarating and grueling. One of our fellow bikers had encouraged me with a Confucius quote, "Our greatest glory is not in never falling, but in rising up every time we fall." I remember thinking on that trip that there were similar parallels to the steady advancement of LGBT rights. It seemed like the movement was gaining momentum and that maybe it was approaching a critical mass. The wheels were in motion.

My mom walked her bike down to the curb. She looked Jackie in the eye and said, "I can do it," but hedged, again saying that if Jackie thought it was a bad idea, she wouldn't do it.

Jackie didn't say a word but got on her own bike.

We waited until there was no traffic coming from either direction, and then Terry placed her feet on the pedals for the first time in eight years. Though her strength may have been returning, her body remained atrophied, her calves the size of an elementary school girl's.

I was down in the road, and Zebby was up on the curb. She was even more nervous than I was. I still had clear memories of Terry before her MS had set in, but for Zebby, Terry's MS had been a reality for nearly all her life.

I put my hand on Terry's shoulder, stabilizing her as she put her foot onto the other pedal.

And then, once again, she did the impossible. After five years in her wheelchair and eight years after her diagnosis, my mom was biking.

Zebby and I were jogging to keep up, but after those first ten yards, Mom was off and we slowed down. It was an incredible moment for all four of us. Zebby was crying, Jackie was crying, Terry was crying, and even I got choked up. As she rounded the corner, Terry was screaming with joy. I clapped and cheered her on, and Zebby collapsed on the grass from a combination of calmed anxiousness and sheer disbelief.

My mom did a loop around our neighborhood and came back to the driveway with tears streaming down her face. The next day at church, my mom told everyone in the congregation that she had biked around the block, and then she lit a candle for joy.

After nearly a decade in the chair, my mom was back on her feet.

THE MERITS OF BRAVERY

In the fall of 2009, I was a freshman at the University of Iowa and often found myself studying at the downtown Java House, a local coffee shop. As I pored through my *Technology and Society* textbook, I noticed that sound engineers were setting up what looked like recording equipment. There were simple, wooden stools on the small stage in the back of the room, a soundboard near the middle, and cables running from the stage to the board.

A motley crew of folks was gathered near the stage, conversing among themselves. Near them was a small sign that read, "The Exchange, with Ben Kieffer." I knew Ben and his radio show, because, well, he's Nic's uncle. (Iowa City often feels like a *very* small town.) I quickly surmised that Ben was interviewing a panel of Tea Party folks—the movement was just starting to gain traction in a big way. It was really the only conceivable situation in which a superslick guy in a three-piece suit, a man wearing a cowboy hat, a young student, a Joe Six-Pack, a female Jerry Falwell, and someone clearly running for Congress could all be on the same stage.

After getting all the equipment set up, the interview commenced, and each of the panelists explained what he or she believed to be his or her own role in the Tea Party, what drew each one to the movement, and the hopes and aspirations that they all shared for the unofficial party's progression. I kept reading—I had a midterm coming up—but kept a small amount of attention on the conversation.

Maybe thirty minutes later, Ben opened up the panel for questions from the audience and callers listening to the broadcast. I had just finished the section I was trying to get through but had a little time to kill before my last class of the day, so I stayed to listen. After some questions about taxes and fiscal policy, I decided to ask one of my own. At this moment I had to summon a good amount of courage to, as we're taught in Scouting, *"Stand for what [I thought was] right even if others laugh at or threaten [me]."*

When Ben called on me, feeling the butterflies in my stomach, I decided to start with the familiar. "My name is Zach. I'm a student here at the university. I'm an Eagle Scout, an entrepreneur, and definitively a capitalist," as one of the panelists had suggested that President Obama was a socialist. A couple of them broke out in wide smiles, laughing, and one even clapped and whooped in support. "I'm not sure if you saw the *Des Moines Register* poll from a few weeks ago, but it said that 92 percent of Iowans didn't feel that the legalization of same-sex marriage had affected their lives. I definitely fall in the other 8 percent because I was thrilled that my lesbian moms were finally able to get legally married. I'm wondering how you feel, and if, as supporters of limited government, you agree with the Supreme Court's ruling."

There was a brief moment of stunned silence as the panel tried to digest my question. The wide enthusiastic smiles at my being a capitalist Eagle Scout were quickly replaced by looks of compassionate concern for my situation. The high school student piped up first, expressing full-throated support for marriage equality. The man in the cowboy hat, a self-identified libertarian, seconded the sentiment.

The rest of the panel looked very, very uncomfortable. Eventually, Joe Six-Pack said that he thought Iowans should get to vote. (A thought later echoed many, many times at the hearing on House Joint Resolution 6.) He was confident in his opinion.

Female Jerry Falwell was clearly wrestling with this conundrum.

"Have you ever met your father?" she asked me.

"No," I replied. "Biologically, my father is an anonymous sperm donor." In another time and place, I might have explained what I believe to be the difference between "father" and "dad." Biologically, *everyone* has a "father," but "dad" is a title that is earned and cemented by an emotional, not genetic, bond.

"Don't you ever long to meet your father? To *have* a father?" she asked, continuing her line of questioning, her face painted in what appeared to be genuine worry for my well-being.

"No, not really," I replied. "I don't think the biological connection is what's important, I think it's really the emotional connection that matters."

In an interesting twist of fate, I would later discover that this same woman would dissect my future testimony on her radio show and suggest that since I had said I thought my full biological connection to my sister was "really cool for me," my own testimony was proof that I was contradicting myself. I doubt, however, that many people today, including twenty-three-time foster mother Michele Bachmann, would actually argue a biological connection trumps an emotional one.

That day, though, she nodded slowly and looked to her fellow Tea Partiers for support. Three-piece Suit promptly looked away without saying a word, and Running for Congress quickly mumbled an expression of support about letting the people vote.

After a few more minutes of questions, the program ended and I decided to stick around. The woman who had been so concerned about my father came up to me to ask some more questions.

"So you've really never met your father?"

"That's right," I said.

"And you said you're an Eagle Scout?"

"I am," I replied. "And actually, my moms were very active in my Scouting experience growing up."

"Hmm," she said, pausing. Then, after a moment, she added, "Well you seem like an attractive, intelligent young man."

Thanks? Yeah. I suppose. I'll take what I can get.

"Thanks," I said with a smile that I'm sure looked a bit strained.

I'm able to stand up and talk to others about my family only because my moms, in turn, had the courage to stand up for their rights when complacency was all too common. Terry was the one who, before she met Jackie, had chosen to pursue motherhood when society told her, "No, this isn't for people like you," and against all odds, succeeded. And it was Jackie who, in the face of a life-changing MS diagnosis and an uncertain future, chose to stand by Terry's side when her doctors told her, "There's no return."

Courage, my mothers taught me, is not the bravado we see on TV and in the movies. Courage, my mothers taught me, is not the absence of fear—it is the *mastery* of fear. Courage is knowing that you're beaten and forging ahead anyway. Gays and lesbians have had to not be truthful about who they are for millennia. Only in the last few decades, as brave men and women courageously came out of the closet and spoke the truth about who they are, has honesty become a safe possibility for most gay people. Courage is Rosa Parks refusing to give up her bus seat in 1955 when the law said the color of her skin determined where she could and could not sit. Courage is the determination of the people at Stonewall Inn in 1969. When the nation said, "You are second-class citizens and are unwelcome in our establishments," they bravely stood up and said, "This is not right." Courage is what drives those who know that, as Voltaire once observed, "It is dangerous to be right when those in power are wrong."

Yet there are so many times in my life that I have stood by silently while people mocked gays or used derogatory slurs that it is hard for me to think that simply delivering my testimony qualifies me as brave. When I consider the many times when I was younger and wanted to defend my parents but was seized by cowardice, I feel cursed now by the words I never said and the fear that stopped me from saying them.

In my pursuit of the security sameness brings, I overlooked the fact that people can, in fact, be different. I am different. My moms are different. My family is different. But the love that unites us all is exactly the same. And it was this realization—and knowing that it didn't matter if I was gay or straight, tall or short, white or black—that allowed me to master my fear. My family might look different—and we are not even recognized as a "real" family by many—but that's okay. Difference is okay. And difference does not disqualify us, or anyone else, from equal protection under the law.

As my Scout handbook says, "Saving lives is not the only test of bravery. You are brave every time you do what is right in spite of what others might say. You are brave when you speak the truth and when you admit a mistake and apologize for it. And you show true courage when you defend the rights of others."

Amen.

Whatever courage I have today was instilled in me by the bravest people I've ever known—my two moms.

CHAPTER 14

❧

"Do a Good Turn Daily"

On April 3, 2009, the Iowa Supreme Court struck down the ban on same-sex marriage in our state in a unanimous ruling on the case of *Varnum v. Brien*. Words cannot describe how I felt. I started playing U2's "Beautiful Day" on my iPod and listened to it for pretty much the rest of that beautiful day. Pardon the colloquialism of a twenty-year-old, but it was, in a word, awesome.

"Equal protection," the Court ruled, "demands that laws treat alike all people who are 'similarly situated with respect to the legitimate purposes of the law.'" When it came to marriage, Iowa could not legally separate gay people from straight people, gay love from straight love. The legal machinations of due process had determined what I already knew to be true: Respect, dignity, and equality ought not be deprived on the basis of sexual orientation.

In the landmark decision, Justice Mark Cady wrote,

"Our responsibility . . . is to protect constitutional rights of individuals from legislative enactments that have denied those rights, even when the rights have not yet been broadly accepted, were at one time unimagined, or challenge a deeply ingrained practice or law viewed to be impervious to the passage of time."

For the couples involved in the *Varnum v. Brien* case, and for many other Iowans including my moms, it was a life-changing ruling. Democratic Senate Majority Leader Mike Gronstal and Iowa House Speaker Pat Murphy expressed a sentiment to which I could well relate, proclaiming in a joint statement, "When all is said and done, we believe the only lasting question about today's events will be why it took us so long."

I immediately called my moms when the news broke, got their voicemail and then headed to school, unable to wipe the grin from my face. When I got to class for my newspaper lab, I sat down and started writing. I had my next column:

As the son of a same-sex couple in Iowa, one of the first test-tube babies of a lesbian mother nationwide, I was elated Friday to learn that the Iowa Supreme Court had unanimously struck down the ban on same-sex marriage in Iowa.

While a majority of Iowans remain opposed to same-sex marriage, and it could be prohibited again with an amendment to the Iowa Constitution, this decision brings Iowa the unique opportunity of setting a national, common-sense precedent.

Instead of trying to protect the right of same-sex

couples to marry, which is political suicide for the fragile Democratic majority, the Iowa General Assembly ought to move to clarify the difference between marriage and civil unions. According to a December 2008 Newsweek poll, a majority of Americans support at least civil unions for same-sex couples. It would take a brave lawmaker, but one ought to propose a piece of legislation to completely remove government from the "marriage process" altogether, leaving a religious ceremony to religious institutions, and make civil unions, accessible by any two people, including those of the same sex, the norm for legal benefits.

Such legislation would not only satisfy strict constructionist conservatives, but would allow the benefits and consequences that we currently associate with marriage to all couples, regardless of sexual orientation.

The election of 2008 swept into office politicians who recognize the normalcy of same-sex couples and their families. It must be realized that the sex of one's parents does not have an unusually profound effect on the life of the child.

I stand as living proof that one can be raised by a same-sex couple, and a couple plagued by the grueling trials of progressive multiple sclerosis at that, and still turn out all right. I have experienced success in speech and debate, journalism, and academics; am politically involved in my community, and have received acceptance to prestigious colleges across the country.

Same-sex parents are not, by definition, unfit to parent, and same-sex families are not, by definition, any more troubled than "regular" families. I have found positive male role models in my life who have set outstanding examples for my own behavior, but the strength demonstrated by my MS-stricken biological mother, Terry, has been surpassed by none I have met. It is with great pride that I call myself her son. And soon, I hope, it will be with great pride that she calls her partner, Jackie, her wife.

The Iowa Supreme Court should be commended for its courage in this decision, but it must be remembered that this is not an end in and of itself. The struggle for true equality will endure, and adopting the civil-union legislation is one of the best ways to continue moving forward.

After our journalism advisor read my piece, she encouraged me to submit it to the *Des Moines Register*, Iowa's largest newspaper. They picked it up and ran it over the weekend in their Sunday issue, which has a circulation of more than 200,000 households across the state. It was a full-circle moment. The journey began with an assigned opinion piece as a freshman that led me to come out for my parents at school. Now I was coming out for my family once more—to the entire state of Iowa. And as full circle as the moment felt, I had no idea that it was just the beginning.

It's funny, because to my family the decision was both a big deal and not really a big deal at all. Our family was our family and we didn't (and don't) feel like we needed validation from the state. Even though my moms weren't married in the eyes of the law, we all knew they'd been married in front of friends, family, and God a long time ago, and that was what mattered to us the most.

On the other hand, as we had experienced and would soon be reminded, the legal rights, privileges, and protections that accompany a legally recognized marriage are most certainly a big deal. My moms wanted a(nother) church wedding and chose October 17, 2009, the fiftieth wedding anniversary of Jackie's parents.

Over the summer, however, amid the onset of the Great Recession, the University of Iowa Hospital and Clinics eliminated Jackie's position as a nurse practitioner. She had ninety days' notice that her job would be over, as would her health insurance unless she paid a hefty monthly premium. My moms' commitment didn't allow for Jackie to be on Terry's family health insurance plan. They decided to be legally wed in August to prevent a lapse in coverage and then have the church service in October as scheduled.

Watching them fill out their marriage license with our minister on a beautiful, hot summer day was really, really cool. Amazing actually. After they crossed their t's and dotted their i's, we headed down to a small garden courtyard in front of our church, where I bore witness to them reexchanging their rings and resaying their I do's.

We went out to lunch at the Atlas, a nice local restaurant. Terry proudly mentioned to the waitress that they had just gotten married. "Well, then," she said, "we need to send you over some champagne!"

From my vantage point, I watched the manager walk out with a bottle of champagne in her hand. She looked around, glancing at our table, and then walked back inside. About a minute later, she came back out and eventually made her way over to our table. I know my moms didn't pick up on it at all, but the manager wasn't pleased and it showed. She clearly wasn't expecting a lesbian couple, but to her credit, she followed through even if she was rather frosty about it.

"They told me you guys just got married," she said, her smile tight. "Congratulations. Here's some champagne." With that, she set the bottle on our table and walked away. We were very happy. After fifteen years as a couple, they were now legitimately wed in Iowa and legally recognized as such.

Life was good.

Yet all was not well in the heartland. Immediately after the ruling in *Varnum v. Brien*, pollsters and journalists began putting their fingers to the wind to try to figure out what Iowans were thinking. Despite numerous polls and dozens of articles, the picture was not clear. Yes, 92 percent of Iowans felt they were unaffected by the ruling, but a solid 43 percent were opposed to the verdict—and its implications—and indicated that they would vote in favor of a constitutional amendment to ban same sex marriage.

Enter Bob Vander Plaats, a then-twice-defeated candidate for the GOP nomination (in 2002 and 2006) for governor of Iowa, who elected to make the *Varnum* decision the focus of what would become his third failed campaign for governor. (He gets points for effort, though!) Mr. Vander Plaats, over the course of several occasions, proclaimed that, were he elected governor, he would issue an executive order to prevent city clerks from issuing marriage licenses to same-sex couples—a move dismissed as political posturing by legal experts who pointed out that governors cannot overrule the Supreme Court.

Even in an election cycle that leaned far to the right, his particular flavor of hard-right conservatism was not appealing to the electorate. Once again defeated in the nomination process, Mr. Vander Plaats turned his focus to the impending retention votes for three members of the Iowa Supreme Court. A retention vote works as a referendum for citizens to remove justices from office in the event of some egregious offense, typically for criminal activity or suspected corruption. The wording on the ballot is simple: "Should Justice X of the Iowa Supreme Court retain her office?" In Iowa, these votes take place every eight years, but from the time the system was adopted in 1962 until 2009, not a single justice had ever been removed from office. In fact, none had ever even come close.

Mr. Vander Plaats changed that.

As I watched the election results pour in on my laptop via Twitter and two live blogs, while I flipped back and forth between MSNBC, Fox News, and CNN, my heart began to drop into my stomach. In unprecedented fashion, Iowans removed from office all three justices.

The campaign had been ugly and one-sided.

The National Organization for Marriage (NOM) had campaigned heavily in our state against retaining the justices. Some church leaders may have breached the rules governing their non-profit, tax-exempt status by strongly encouraging their parishioners to vote against retention. Outside money from far-right conservative groups rushed into the state. When the dust had settled, more than 95 percent of the money spent against retaining the judges came from outside the state, and interestingly, nearly 95 percent of the money spent to retain the justices came from inside the state. More to the point, opponents to retention spent more than twice what those in support of retention did. External forces, without question, shaped the race.

Further, the GOP reclaimed a majority in the Iowa House, Republican Terry Branstad was back in the governor's mansion and the Democratic majority in the Senate had been cut to the smallest possible margin, of 26–24. I didn't need tea leaves to know that the political onslaught would be fast and fierce.

As I sat on my couch, unsure of how to respond, what to do or what to say, it became clear that there was a good chance—a very good chance—that marriage equality in Iowa was not as secure as we had all hoped. In our rush to celebrate our progress and good fortune, we had neglected to do the work of securing our gains, ignoring the long slog of winning hearts and minds.

We thought we had been sprinting through the finish, but the 2010 election was a somber reminder that this was just another mile marker in the marathon. We were now on defense, the momentum had swung back to the other side and they wasted no time making the most of it.

Within a week of convening the eighty-fourth Iowa General Assembly—which has a two-year legislating period that is similar to that of the U.S. Congress—the Iowa House Judiciary Committee approved House Joint Resolution 6, which began the process of amending the Iowa Constitution to redefine marriage as between one man and one woman. The constitutional amendment would also specifically deny same-sex couples the possibility of civil unions as a legal alternative to marriage. Due to the immense public interest in the matter, the committee decided to host a public hearing.

In such forums, both the Republicans and Democrats invite the first five speakers from which they hope to hear testimony. The Democrats tapped One Iowa, the state's largest LGBT advocacy organization, to secure those five speakers. A staff member at Lambda Legal, One Iowa's legal partner, remembered my 2009 column in the *Register* about growing up with two moms and asked me if I could make it. Lambda Legal is one of the foremost legal organizations advancing LGBT rights in this country, having litigated the landmark *Lawrence v. Texas* case, in which the U.S. Supreme Court struck down so-called antisodomy laws. I was flattered to have been approached by such a storied group, but I told their communications director that I'd see if I could find someone else to babysit in my stead, as I was slated to watch the kids of my friends Sara and Erica.

Needless to say, we found another babysitter.

Here's the thing. I could walk you through all the explanations about why same-sex marriage should be legal and go through due process and explain equal protection doctrine and the first and fourteenth amendments. I could review the scientific literature explaining that homosexuality is not a choice, that it is not a psychological disorder, that it has zero effect on a person's capacity to rear children and on and on. I could sit down with you and go tit for tat until both our throats are sore. At the end of the day, however, a person can't be reasoned out of something he or she wasn't reasoned into, so I'll simply observe that ultimately this is a conversation about marriage, and marriage is two things: love and commitment. There is something fundamentally human, neither gay nor straight, about the universal desire to both love and be loved.

Even before my moms were actually married, they were in love. Even before they actually had all of the legal rights, privileges, protections, and responsibilities inherent in civil marriage, they were committed. Love is responsibility. Love is respect. Love is courage, kindness, faith, discipline, and honesty. Love, I once read, is giving somebody the power to destroy you and trusting them not to. Love is the sum total of the values I learned from my two moms.

I was sixteen years old when I watched Jackie hold Terry in her arms, Terry whimpering from the uncontrollable pain of MS and Jackie sobbing because there was nothing she could do. I realized then, as I stood in the doorway as a helpless observer, that it is the people who try to break love down and compartmentalize it and rationalize it who think that straight love is different from gay love is different from interracial love. It is the people who think that love can be understood who are least capable of doing so.

Kurt Vonnegut, my favorite author, once wrote, "There's only one rule that I know of, babies—: 'God damn it, you've got to be kind.'" He passed in 2007, but his words survive, and I think there's something to that rule. It's a sentiment found in religious texts of all kinds and the root of many philosophical schools of thought. To be kind is to demonstrate respect. It's to engage with a fellow human being and, with your actions, show that person that you believe he or she is as valuable as you are.

I wish there was more kindness on both sides of the marriage equality debate. All too often gay people are demonized and treated poorly by people opposed to their "lifestyle choice." And all too often opponents of same-sex marriage are dismissed as ignorant or bigoted or hateful. The truth is, it's just not that simple.

On my way to a recent event in Los Angeles, I found myself explaining why I was in L.A. to the driver. He was a well-built, forty-two-year-old Brazilian man with salt-and-pepper hair, who moved to the United States when he was twenty-one to pursue his dream of becoming a U.S. fighter pilot. Unable to get a green card, he went to flight school for nonmilitary pilots and now spends his days flying private jets and running his own personal chauffeur service.

He was frank in the way he talked about his views on gay marriage and homosexuality. Growing up in strictly Catholic Brazil, the very notion of gay marriage did not even exist, and needless to say, the concept was not up for debate. He listened carefully and intently as I explained what brought me to L.A., a description that called for an explanation of my family situation. He nodded along, and then said, "You see, seeing two mans together, it's very aggressive to me. Two womans, not as much, but still a little. They don't match, in my mind."

As we talked, calmly and civilly, it became clear that despite his discomfort with homosexuality, he was not willing to go so far as to inflict his views and beliefs on his fellow human beings if he could not see any danger or harm posed by families like mine. He had listened to the arguments and was still not convinced that homosexuality was right, per se, but nor could he believe that, despite his feeling that "they do not match," gay men and women should be deprived of their rights—he would respect them.

And to be honest, that's all I ask. Winston Churchill once said, "Courage is what it takes to stand up and speak; courage is also what it takes to sit down and listen." I find this wisdom to be particularly powerful given my sudden involvement in this movement, and I remember it as a reminder to close my mouth and open my ears when appropriate.

This country has had great debates in the past—about the original revolution, slavery, the Great Depression, women's rights, Jim Crow laws, the Cold War—and we got through them all because enough people respected one another and were wiling to sit down and talk it through. But these debates didn't happen in Washington, D.C., or the mass media. Though the media may have covered these debates, they didn't take place in the newspapers or over the radio or on nightly television broadcasts. These debates were composed of cogent conversations between and among friends and families, neighbors and parishioners, coworkers and teammates, drivers and passengers. Simple as they may be, these conversations moved this country forward.

I believe that we all possess the power to shape the narrative that describes the human condition. Such sculpture is not necessarily for what we each believe to be the better. What I view as liberation may, to another, be seen as oppression. But the inscription of our values on the arc of history comes with a responsibility that cannot be taken lightly. As fiercely as you and I may believe what we believe, we must also recognize the autonomy and dignity of those around us and those affected by our choices.

Darkness cannot extirpate darkness, just as hate has no hope of ever erasing hate. Only light, love, and tolerance—even, and particularly, of those with whom we most disagree—have a prayer of doing that.

A month after my moms' public wedding, I decided it was time for me to start giving back, to do my good turn, so to speak. I decided to attend an event for LGBT families in Des Moines called "Around the Table." It was hosted by the organizations One Iowa and Lambda Legal to help same-sex couples (and a wide spectrum of lesbian, gay, bisexual, and transgender folks) answer questions about the ruling and learn more about what they could do to help keep the momentum moving forward. I drove our minivan out to Des Moines, parked on a street in downtown, and actually slept in it, camping out in the trunk. I was there to work with the kids of LGBT couples in attendance—pretty much a glorified babysitter.

The night before everyone arrived, there was a dinner and I received some basic training on how to talk about family-related questions with kids. I met a girl my age who also has two moms. We hit it off immediately and remain friends to this day. But the reason we hit it off wasn't because we both have two moms; it was because she was interesting and funny and liked sci-fi almost as much as I did. The fact that we both have gay parents is certainly a component of our friendship, but it is by no means defining.

We got to work with these kids who were all pretty young, most of them probably about seven or eight. I'm not a particularly emotional guy, but I got choked up listening to these kids talking about their experiences. There were some who didn't even realize that they had gay parents. In their words, they "just have two moms." I remember this one little kid who didn't understand why he was even there. So normal was his life experience that it wasn't until after lunch that he came back and said, "Oh, yeah, I am one of those."

Another young boy who had two mothers was very confused and got pretty upset. He said he was very sad about why people were opposed to gay marriage. He couldn't comprehend why some people didn't want his moms to get married. He didn't understand how it could *not* be okay. He kept saying his family was normal. I looked in his eyes and could see his genuine concern. He believed that kids from families run by gay couples were really—in every single way that mattered—not any different from families run by heterosexual people.

Then it dawned on me as this boy talked: I was normal until society told me they didn't think I was normal. I realized that the little kid looking up at us, with his brown hair, large eyes, and big smile, was me.

My heart went out to him, because I knew that at some point in his life he was going to come face-to-face with people who didn't want him to exist, who thought he would need "fixing." I knew the pain he was going to feel. He was the naive third grader who hadn't yet been asked, "What do your mom and dad do?"

Opponents will often talk about the struggles and challenges that children of gay couples have to go through. I will say only this: We have to go through those challenges because you put us through them. We only have to experience that pain because you insist on inflicting it. By trying to tell us that there is something wrong with gay marriage, that there is something wrong with families led by gay couples, you create something wrong—*you* become the source of our pain.

Knowing the challenges that little boy will have to face and the things he will have to deal with—that we're still not at a point when he can live a childhood untouched by fear and unsullied by hate—breaks my heart.

This book is for him.

AFTERWORD

The struggle to obtain civil marriage equality for same-sex couples has been an interesting—and often surprising—lesson in American politics.

I was sitting in a hotel room in Burlington, Vermont, answering e-mails during the middle of the book tour for *My Two Moms*. The LED on my smartphone was blinking. Looking at my notifications, I started to see a ton of buzz on Twitter about an impending White House interview with the president about an undisclosed subject.

In a sit-down conversation specifically to address the issue, President Obama announced he was endorsing same-sex marriage, describing recognition of relationships like my moms' as "the right thing to do." In doing so, our first-ever black president *also* became our first-ever sitting president to endorse civil marriage equality. Citing, among other things, some friends of his daughters who were the children of same-sex couples, he said that they disproved many of the misconceptions about same-sex parents. He also spoke of the Young Republicans on college campuses pushing him to support marriage equality.

I didn't believe it. Despite an outstanding bet with two conservative friends of mine that President Obama would endorse same-sex marriage before the 2012 Democratic Convention, I was still shocked when it actually happened. Before the interview was even over, I was on the phone with Terry to ask her if she knew what was going on. "Have I heard, wait, what?" she asked. "What are you talking about?"

"He's endorsing same-sex marriage!" I told her. "Like, right now. Turn on ABC."

"Is he *crazy*?" she yelled. "That's suicide!"

It wasn't suicide.

On November 6, 2012, not only was President Obama reelected by a 126 electoral vote spread, he became only the third president in the last hundred years to win with a majority of the popular vote in back-to-back elections. The other two were presidents Franklin Roosevelt and Dwight Eisenhower. Further, the president led his party in wholeheartedly embracing the recognition of same-sex marriage. I had the incredible opportunity to personally hear his historic second inaugural address, in which he described the protests at Stonewall in the same breath as the women's rights summit at Seneca Falls and the Selma Voting Rights Movement. It appears near certain that future Democratic presidential candidates will continue President Obama's support for LGBT rights.

The struggle to obtain civil marriage equality for same-sex couples has been a long and interesting lesson in American (and even international) politics. The argument deployed again and again by those opposed to such equality was that we (the voters) would *never* vote to recognize same-sex unions, that such recognition would be forced upon us by unelected, tyrannical judges. They told us *real* Americans would never recognize *homosexual* relationships. They told us this day would never come. "Not in America," they said.

They were wrong.

At their 2012 convention in Charlotte, North Carolina, the Democratic Party highlighted its commitment to LGBTQ rights—on the night the president spoke no less—and I was invited to speak there, once more, about my mothers. Unlike the night in Des Moines, I knew I was being recorded. I understood the gravity of the moment—more than 20,000 people in the auditorium and millions more watching live on television at home.

I was nervous backstage, shaking with excitement and emotion that I suppose was both a combination of eagerness and terror—related, I'm sure in retrospect, to the fact that I had just bumped into Scarlett Johansson. As I walked to the podium, the audience roared in approval. During my speech, as I set straight the lies (no pun intended) that had been told about families like mine during the GOP convention in 2004, I had to pause numerous times as the crowd broke out in thunderous applause and cheer. I walked off stage, my moms told me, to a standing ovation.

A friend later remarked it was likely the first time anyone had spoken in prime time at a major party's convention as the result of a YouTube video.

Not bad.

As I've traveled all over the country speaking, campaigning, and advocating for other children of same-sex parents, I have continued to be surprised, over and over again, at the response people have to *the* YouTube video and to me personally. It has become clear that to many I have become less a person and more a symbol—a testament to the ability of same-sex couples to raise children and an example of what can happen when truth is spoken to power.

This realization has given me much perspective and continues to remind me of why it's so important to remember who I am, where I come from, and why I am where I am. It is a realization for which I am deeply and profoundly grateful. My family and I—and indeed a majority of the citizens of this nation—are once more part of the effort to bend the arc of the moral universe toward justice.

There's no going back. We stand on the right side of history.

We stand on the side of love.

ACKNOWLEDGMENTS

Douglas Adams once wrote: "I may not have gone where I intended to go, but I think I have ended up where I needed to be." This is a sentiment to which I can well relate.

There are so many places along the journey that brought this book to fruition, where the entire thing could have been derailed, that the odds of it actually coming to pass seemed astronomical. But here we are.

Thank you, Jackie and Terry. I love both of you more than I'll ever be able to express, and I am grateful beyond measure for the lessons, love, and strength you've instilled in me.

Thank you, Zebby. I can't believe that you are now a college student. Good Lord. It's with a mix of pride and terror that I've watched you grow into a beautiful young woman. You're going to do amazing things.

Thank you, Nic (and the rest of the Jewell/Kieffer clan), for keeping my feet on the ground when my head is in the clouds. Your friendship has meant the world to me.

Thank you, Mitch and Melanie, for being there when I needed you most and for all of your help since.

Thank you, John and Ilyse, for your unending support, guidance, friendship, and wonderful, wonderful food.

Thank you, President Obama, OFA, and the DNC, for inviting me to speak at the 2012 Democratic National Convention in Charlotte. I had a blast, and it was with great heart and pride that I cheered your reelection.

Thank you, Leah, Richard, Kate, Jake, and Andrew, for an incredible week in Minnesota. I am so, so proud to have been a part of the campaign and was absolutely elated—right along with you—when the AP called the race. On to the next one.

Thank you to all of the mentors and teachers I've had along the way: Mrs. Keech, Ms. Secrist, Mr. Smith, Joe Brisben, Mr. Lawson, Ms. Swenson, Ms. Shullaw, Mr. Steward, Mike Carroll, Ms. Ohlmann, the Davis brothers, Ms. Meinel, Brez, and Dr. Arganbright, to name but a few.

Thank you, Scott and Lisa, for showing me that "conservative" does not mean "close-minded."

Thank you to Ellen DeGeneres, Perez Hilton, Ashton Kutcher, Rosie O'Donnell, Lawrence O'Donnell, Thomas Roberts, Rachel Maddow, Neil Patrick Harris, Chelsea Handler, George Takei, and Melissa Etheridge for lending me the strength of your voices and passions.

Thank you to the Boy Scouts of America for underscoring the importance of the values my mothers taught me.

Thank you to Lisa Hardaway, Camilla Taylor, Christopher Clark, Kevin Cathcart, and everyone else at Lambda Legal—and all of the plaintiffs, especially Kate and Trish—who made the *Varnum* ruling possible.

Thank you to Iowa senator Mike Gronstal for standing firm and refusing to put my mothers' right to marriage up to a vote. You are truly a statesman.

Thank you, also, to all of the national groups—Human

Rights Campaign, Family Equality Council, Freedom to Marry, and COLAGE, among countless more—for continuing their relentless and often thankless work of advancing, securing, and protecting LGBT rights across the country.

On a more personal note, I'd like to thank Emily Schlichting, Ben Geyerhahn, Jill Strauss, Jamie Citron, Zachary Allen, Anna Ruch, Zach Koutsky, Kenny Sunshine, Jay Strell, Brian Ellner, Cathy Renna, Lindsay Gordon, Lisa Johnson, Laura Dawn, Eli Praiser, Lou Pizzitola, the Iowa House Democrats, and Sy Presten for your generosity and assistance.

Thank you, also, to everyone who watched *the* video, who shared it on Facebook, retweeted it on Twitter, upvoted it on Reddit, showed it to a class or family. This new era of social media is a persuasive reminder of the power we all have to shape the world for the better.

Thank you, William Shinker, Megan Newman, Travers Johnson, and Rachel Holtzman, for seeing what this book could be and for guiding it to publication.

Thank you to JL Stermer, my incredible, relentless literary agent for believing both in me and in this story. Here's to the first of many.

When I sat down to write this book, a friend of mine remarked, "You know, maybe there's something to destiny." I laughed it off. I don't believe in fate. Having just finished the manuscript, however, I can't help but wonder if maybe Scott was on to something. I suppose it's hard to say at this point, but regardless, thank you, Scott. And thank you, Bruce. The last two years have been incredible, and without you I wouldn't be where (or who, even) I am today. It's been one hell of a ride—and we're just getting started.

⌘

The Twelve Questions
I'm Asked Most Frequently

1. *Are you gay?*

If you're still wondering about this after reading the book, you must have skipped a few passages or have very selective memories. Otherwise you're standing in a bookstore and flipped right to this section. Either way, you totally missed the point of this whole book. Whether or not I'm gay, straight, or bisexual; tall or short; male or female; white or black; cisgender or transgender; successful go-getter or pot-smoking slacker; is entirely immaterial.

It might be a shocker, but I do in fact know a couple of kids who have gay parents who are themselves gay. (But I should also point out that straight parents have been the leading cause of gay people for just about forever.) I happen to be a go-getter student-turned-activist speaking out in defense of his moms, but this isn't—and shouldn't be—the norm.

Nobody wants to spend all of his time defending his family, and I'm looking forward to a time when mine no longer need defending. That being said, I answer this question in the book, so I suggest you go back and find the answer there. You'll feel like a regular Sherlock Holmes when you figure it out!

2. *Which one of your moms is the man?*

I've actually been asked this a number of times, and almost every time I crack up laughing, mostly because I have a hard time imagining either one of my moms as "the man," so to speak. I usually explain it with a funny analogy I read on the Internet. Asking which one of my moms is the man is a lot like walking into a Chinese restaurant and asking which chopstick is the fork. That's just not how it works—it's a whole different set of utensils.

3. *Isn't it different, growing up with lesbian parents?*

When people ask me this question, I've figured out that they're not actually asking about what it's like growing up with gay parents. On an intuitive level, I think we almost all know that there isn't a huge difference. After all, gay people have been raising children since the beginning of our species— it's not like homosexuality was created during the sixties by free love and weed. There have been gay people for as long as there have been Homo sapiens, it's just that recently gay people have been able to raise children and start families with someone of the same sexual orientation. So the question isn't actually, "What's it like growing up with lesbian parents," it's, "What is it like growing up as a man without a father?"

4. What's it like growing up as a man without a father?

Good question! I'm glad you asked. I think it's useful to point out that I do, in fact, have a biological father, just like everybody else on this planet, but I don't have a dad. I think of "father" as the genetic connection and "dad" as the emotional connection. I've got a few friends who were adopted—some immediately after birth, some a few years later—but to all of them, their moms and dads, though not their biological parents, are the people with whom they have emotional connections. Love is what makes a family—not genetics.

So, as far as growing up without a dad goes, I'm guessing that my experience wasn't much different from guys raised by single mothers, of which there are many. President Bill Clinton, Lance Armstrong, Jon Stewart, and Samuel L. Jackson all grew up with minimal or no contact with their fathers. They all turned out just fine, obviously. Of course, on the flip side, Saddam Hussein and John Wilkes Booth didn't have dads in much of their lives, either. So I think that just goes to show what little of an effect it has one way or the other.

I had to learn how to shave from a friend's dad. It wasn't a big deal. But, as I hope I've illustrated in this book, I didn't need a dad to teach me values. My moms had that covered, from self-discipline, courage, and perseverance to kindness, patience, and friendliness. I'll simply finish with the observation that anyone who thinks women are incapable of teaching their children about values like self-discipline and courage clearly doesn't know much about the women in his life.

5. *Don't you ever long to meet your donor?*

Nope. Would it be interesting to talk with him over a pitcher of beer? Sure. Do I have a burning desire to find him? No. Am I grateful he donated? Absolutely.

6. *How did having lesbian moms affect your dating life?*

If anything, it's been beneficial. I learned "womanese" pretty quickly, which has made communication infinitely easier. I'm also really good at putting the seat down, which I've been told is kind of a big deal. Some people have asked me if I have difficulty being "the man" in the relationship. First off, I think that's a really dated concept, and it feels like an out-of-place question for the twenty-first century. That being said, I'm still a pretty aggressive guy and don't hesitate to call someone (including a significant other) out on his or her bullshit if I feel like I'm being played.

Like all guys (and girls), learning about dating has been a lot of trial and error for me, but anyone who suggests that kids raised by gay parents are the only ones who don't immediately know how the impossibly complex mating ritual we call "dating" works is kidding him- or herself.

7. *What about your friendships with other guys?*

As I pointed out in my testimony, nobody has ever come to the independent realization that a lesbian couple raised me. While, personally, I'm fairly introverted and run with a pretty tight circle of friends, I've never run into any problems in my relationships with other guys. When I was younger, I'd sometimes overreact to pranks. (One time in high school, Nic and

Mike pushed a dead turkey through the back window of my pickup truck, and I damn near blew a gasket.) But, like all guys, I've grown up and matured quite a bit since high school.

I've also never had much trouble with my relationships in a group setting, either. I've been the member or leader of a lot of teams or organizations—sports, speech and debate, Boy Scouts, among others—and never encountered any problems relating to people that I could attribute to the sexuality of my moms.

8. Do you really believe the sexuality of your parents has had zero effect on the content of your character, and not a positive one?

Yes. I've actually caught a lot of flak for that last line of my testimony from folks on the left, who all argued that the sexuality of my parents had a *positive* effect on my life. I don't think this is the case at all, and my moms and sister all agree. Some might say I'm playing a game of semantics, but, having met a lot of gay people, I'll observe that a person's sexuality doesn't tell you that much about the person.

A lot of gay people stay in the closet for their entire lives and fall into self-loathing for any number of reasons. Is that response determined by their sexuality? No, of course not. But would they have to stay in the closet or be self-loathing if they weren't gay? No, they wouldn't. This is the difference: Being gay and how you respond to being gay doesn't shape your character—it reveals your character. The same is true of multiple sclerosis, my mom's disability. My moms' reactions to being gay were determined by the content of their characters, which were shaped by their parents and friends and the environments in which they grew up. Likewise, their parenting wasn't shaped *by the fact* that they were gay; their parenting, too, was determined by the content of their character.

That being said, were they perhaps more sensitive to other forms of persecution or discrimination because they had faced such prejudice in their own lives? Sure. But that doesn't change the fact that they could have reacted to that prejudice with anger or malice or loathing independently of why they were experiencing that discrimination in the first place. My moms' reactions—and their decision to foster values of acceptance and tolerance in my sister and me—were not rooted in the fact that they were gay; they were rooted in the fact that they were both good people who had had good influences in their own lives growing up.

When Zebby and I were young, my moms spent a lot of time researching how to be good parents, not because they were lesbians, but because they wanted to be the best parents they could be. And I'll say they might not have been perfect, but they were pretty damn close.

9.   Who were your male role models growing up?
As much as I hate to admit it, growing up as a Green Bay Packers fan, Brett Favre was an idol of mine for a while. I'm proud to report, however, that that adoration promptly gave way to a profound respect and admiration for Aaron Rodgers. The Packers actually won Super Bowl XLV the Sunday after I testified before the Iowa House Judiciary Committee. Maybe I should testify before governmental bodies more often.

I also want to point out that my moms didn't elope to some all-female compound in Lesbiastan or anything. (And, sorry guys, I've consulted with the Homosexual High Council, and there's no such place.) It would have taken some pretty serious effort for me not to have a lot of contact with men growing up. I had plenty of role models among the dads of my friends, the leaders in my Cub Scout packs and Boy Scouts troop, and my K–12 teachers.

More to the point, however, my moms instilled in me the values of being a good person, which, call me crazy, seems much more meaningful than being a "good man" or "good woman."

10. What's it like being named Salon's second sexiest man of 2011?

To be honest, I was expecting it to have a dramatic effect on my love life, which hasn't yet materialized, but otherwise, yeah, it's pretty awesome.

Just kidding. Well, I mean, it is awesome, but here's the actual tenth question.

10. How would you feel if a gay couple adopted your own child or children?

I'd want to make sure that the couple was committed to raising damn good children, was going to be there for the kids, and understood that it takes a lot of blood, sweat, toil, and tears to successfully sculpt children from little hellions into well-adjusted young adults. But would I have reservations about a gay couple raising my children because they were gay? No. Absolutely not.

**11. *Do you play basketball/Are you taller since the
last time I saw you?***

No and no.

**12. *The Boy Scouts of America publicly states that
homosexual conduct is inconsistent with the
obligations in the Scout oath and law. It bars
agnostics and atheists from participating in the
organization and refuses to allow gays and non-
believers to hold leadership positions. How can
you continue to support, and speak so highly of,
the organization?***

This is an important question. The United States federal government does not yet recognize the validity of same-sex unions
and, indeed, actively discriminates against them. The same is
not true of atheists and agnostics, but there's no doubt that a
culture of religiosity dominates American politics and law.

At a national level, the Boy Scouts of America does indeed discriminate against gays, atheists, and agnostics, but
the implementation of national policy is left to the discretion
of local packs and troops. In my experience, and I understand
that mine is not universal, the folks I met couldn't have cared
less about the sexual orientation of my parents, or me for that
matter. I am not willing, however, to discard my entire experience, the lessons I learned, and the values I lived because of
two flaws in the organization.

Better, I think, is to work toward reshaping those policies, and I hope this book plays some part in the changing of
the guard. Personally I am strongly opposed to the disenfranchisement of gays, atheists, and agnostics by the Boy Scouts

of America and am committed to making sure that such old-fashioned, close-minded policies do not render a valuable organization irrelevant to future generations.

Just as I have no plans on emigrating from the United States because of its refusal to recognize my moms' marriage, I have no plans on distancing myself from the Boy Scouts because of its refusal to acknowledge the validity of my moms' relationship. After all, it was my gay moms who taught me and my fellow Scouts to help other people at all times and to keep myself physically strong, mentally awake, and morally straight.

In addition to my political work (and despite my publisher's sage refusal to let me title this book *My Two Moms—or Everything I Need to Know about Gay Marriage I Learned in the Boy Scouts*), I've continued to stay active in the push to end the Boy Scouts of America's anti-gay membership policy, launching the organization Scouts for Equality. While there is still much work to be done, I am quite optimistic—especially given marriage equality's recent success at the ballot box—about the impending end of this archaic and hurtful policy.

—∽—

The Debate

RESOLVED: THAT SAME-SEX MARRIAGE OUGHT TO BE
LEGALIZED.

OR: A BRIEF SELECTION OF COMMON ARGUMENTS
AGAINST SAME-SEX MARRIAGE AND REBUTTALS TO
THEM.

"I have an idea! If you don't like a constitutional ban, then leave. Stop spending your money here, stop spending your tax dollars here. This country is a republic, and constitutions are the supreme law of the land."

In a lot of different situations and in various contexts, this is actually a really good point. The fact that we have fifty different states means that there are fifty entirely separate sets of laws governing the lives of this country's citizens. If you disagree with tax law in one state, feel free to move to another one. This is perfectly legitimate.

What's really the question here, however, is whether or not the law is unjust. It's unlikely that the aforementioned tax law was unjust; more likely it was just unfavorable to whomever happened to be living there. When a law is unjust, there exists an obligation to change that law.

What makes bans on same-sex marriage unjust is that they deprive American citizens of their constitutionally protected right to civil marriage—a right the U.S. Supreme Court has ruled to be a *right* as opposed to a privilege—which violates equal protection under the law and the right to due process.

If folks who are opposed to same-sex marriage can show, in a court of law and through the use of due process, why the act of two men or two women entering into a civil marriage should be illegal, then it does become a question of unfavorable instead of unjust. Until that time, however, this remains a question of equal protection and civil rights, and thus "just leaving" should not be considered a suitable alternative to changing an unjust law.

"Well, I just don't think government should be involved in marriage!"

Honestly, I agree. If it were up to me, what's commonly known as a "marriage license" would be known as a "civil union." People would still get married in churches or mosques or temples or synagogues or wherever they'd like, but the marriage would be separately and exclusively a religious ceremony. If they want the civil and legal rights, protections, privileges, and responsibilities that come with a civil "marriage," then they can go to the county recorder's office and get a civil union, much like a couple would today to get a marriage license.

However this change would require a substantial change in our social mind-set, and it's unfair to say that the LGBT rights movement should be responsible for that shift. (The same could have been said of interracial couples, and I think we can all recognize that that isn't fair.) I suspect that if civil unions do become the norm, LGBT couples wouldn't be particularly surprised, but if civil unions are going to be put forth as an alternative to marriage *only* for gay couples, I think we can all agree that that's a pretty blatant case of "separate but equal." And we've already tried that in this country. ("Colored" water fountains, anyone?) It doesn't work, and it isn't right.

More than anything else, just blindly switching to civil unions doesn't make much sense. When was the last time you heard someone propose, "Will you civil union me?"

"Marriage is a privilege, therefore we have the right to define who does and who doesn't qualify to be married."

Most immediately, marriage is not in fact a privilege. Let's be clear: The U.S. Supreme Court has ruled that civil marriage is a civil right—most prominently in the unanimous, landmark decision of *Loving v. Virginia*, as the court wrote, "[m]arriage is one of the 'basic civil rights of man.'"

That being said, this is a constitutional republic, and we do have a right to define who does and doesn't qualify for rights. This is, obviously, why we can lock some people away in prison. You break the law, you lose your rights. But we also have equal protection under the law. So before you can deprive people of their rights (i.e., lock them in prison or prevent someone from marrying another person) you have to show in a court of law and through the use of due process *why* that person should be deprived of his or her rights (e.g., broken some law).

This is where opponents of same-sex marriage fall short. If they could demonstrate some negative effect that homosexuality has on other people, if they could show that homosexuality is immoral in a way that does not rely on religious belief (we have, after all, freedom of religion in this country), if they could show that homosexuality has an adverse effect on kids or is somehow unhealthy, if they could show how gay marriage destroys the sanctity of straight marriage, then there would be grounds for deprivation of those rights.

None of these things have ever been proven in a court of law. In fact, in *Perry v. Schwarzenegger*, when the attorney defending California's ban on gay marriage was pressed by the judge to identify how a gay marriage would negatively affect a straight marriage, all he could muster was, "I don't know. I don't know."

"We don't need to have citations to prove the notion that homosexuality is associated with heightened health risks. It's undeniable and widely acknowledged, for instance, that there is a far higher rate of HIV infection among the gay male demographic than the general population."

When folks do find themselves trying to convince others that there is a good, nonreligious reason to argue that homosexuality is dangerous or immoral, this is the one that they often turn to. Being gay, the argument goes, puts you at risk for contracting dangerous diseases like HIV/AIDS, which is a heightened health risk and thus means that it should be discouraged by law, including the deprivation of the right of civil marriage.

This actually seems like a good argument at face value. But as soon as you start digging beneath the surface, it falls apart really quickly. After all, clearly homosexuality *itself* isn't what's causing HIV/AIDS. If a gay person is just sitting on her couch feeling sexual attraction to another woman, she's not going to somehow come down with one of the deadliest autoimmune diseases ever. But if a man who has HIV/AIDS has unprotected sex with another man (or another woman, for that matter) then that person is at a pretty high risk of contracting it.

So if you step back and look at the situation, it's pretty clear that unprotected sex is what causes increased rates of HIV/AIDS, not homosexuality. Further, it's simply a medical reality that engaging in anal sex increases the likelihood of transmitting an STI—and that means *any* STI, not just HIV/AIDS. This is why *homosexual women* are in fact the least likely demographic of people in America to contract HIV/AIDS. They're not having a whole lot of anal sex.

Interestingly, people who put forth the argument that being gay leads to increased rates of HIV/AIDS and therefore gay people shouldn't be able to get married seem to be only looking at what's happening in America and are blatantly ignoring the rest of the world.

In Africa homosexuality is even more taboo than it is here. In many countries homosexual intercourse is punishable by death. Extraordinarily few gay people are out, let alone living the homosexual lifestyle, that some here in America are arguing is responsible for the proliferation of HIV/AIDS. Yet it's also a medical reality that HIV/AIDS rates in Africa are dangerously high. So what gives?

Anal sex. Because condoms are so difficult to come by in Africa, many *straight* couples turn to anal sex in an effort to avoid pregnancy. And they're having anal sex in the first place because they don't have condoms, so obviously it's unprotected. So by the logic of this argument—that because gay men are more likely to engage in a type of unprotected sex that leads to increased rates of HIV/AIDS, they shouldn't be able to marry—marriage between straight people should be illegal in Africa.

Seems kind of obvious once you stop to really think it through. Unfortunately most people just hear "anal sex" or "HIV/AIDS" or "gay people" and shut down. I can understand why some people feel uncomfortable thinking about these topics, but if you're going to vote away the rights of your fellow citizens, your discomfort with anal sex is really not the important thing here.

"This is an assault on the rights of Christians to live and worship!"

I'll let Stephen Colbert and Jon Stewart handle it from here:

Jon Stewart: "I have to say, as someone who is not Christian, it's hard for me to believe Christians are a persecuted people in America. God willing, maybe one of you will even rise up and get elected to be president of this country—or maybe forty-four in a row. But that's my point, is they've taken this idea of no establishment as persecution, because they feel entitled, not to equal status, but to greater status."

Stephen Colbert: "It is well-known that the homosexual

agenda is just an insidious plot to prevent gay teenagers from dying. . . . The point is, bullying is just fine as long as you get a permission slip from God. With this amendment to the law, if you're a Michigan Christian teenager giving a gay kid a swirlie, you can just say it's a baptism."

"Your speech didn't make any logical sense. It was all emotion, and obviously you, as one exception, don't prove that all kids raised by gay parents turn out okay."

My response to this charge has two parts. At the first, there's no doubt that I made a lot of emotional appeals. It's an emotional topic. The Iowa House Judiciary Committee had voted to literally redefine the law with the explicit purpose of preventing couples like my moms from getting married. I was feeling a lot of emotions. But to contend that an argument is somehow invalid because it tugs at our heartstrings or makes some other appeal to emotion is to ignore millennia of arguments. Human beings are emotional creatures, and to deny the role emotions play in our decision-making is to deny a large part of what makes us human.

Second, the response that I'm only one kid and one example doesn't prove that all gay couples are capable of raising children might seem like a good counterpoint, but it fails to take into account the nature of the argument *I* was responding to. That argument goes like this:

1. *Homosexuality is less moral than heterosexuality.*

2. *Therefore gay people are less moral than straight people.*

3. *Because gay people are less moral than straight people, they are less good at raising children.*

4. *Because raising children is an important part of marriage, gay people should not be able to get married.*

5. *Therefore gay marriage should be illegal.*

If opponents of gay marriage are willing to concede that I turned out to be a healthy, successful kid, then this does, in fact, present significant problems to the above argument precisely because of how it is structured. The argument, after all, doesn't contend that *some* gay people are less moral than straight people. It doesn't stipulate that *some* gay couples can successfully raise kids. It does the exact opposite. Gay couples are incapable of successfully raising children *because they are gay.* It's not even a correlation argument, such as saying gay couples are less successful at raising children because a gay person is much more likely to have HIV/AIDS. It's a causation argument, and causation arguments are extraordinarily difficult to defend. Even one, single example of a person overcoming the effects of gravity would be cause to call into question the entire theory of gravity, because gravity applies to everyone. Similarly even one, single example of a kid "overcoming" the effects of gay parents—presuming that his parents are actually gay—calls into question the entire argument that gay parents are incapable of raising children.

If the argument were *some* gay parents are incapable of raising children, then, yes, my one example wouldn't be worth anything. *But that's not the argument.* The argument holds that there is something intrinsic in homosexuality that renders homosexual people less moral, and therefore less capable of parenting. Were the argument to be that only *some* gay people are less capable of raising children, you would have a much stronger argument that would be more difficult to disprove. But then, logically, you'd also have to recognize that if morality is a condition of marriage, not all straight parents are moral. Some, in fact, are serial adulterers, and after each successive affair, they can get remarried. But my moms, who have been together since 1995? No. Not them.

"What about the children! Kids deserve both a mother and a father."

First off, this is a silly argument considering that it comes from the people who say that government shouldn't be intervening in the lives of its citizens. After all, does the government intervene and take kids away from single parents when the mother or father dies and then hold on to them until the remaining parent finds a new partner? No, of course not. Is it illegal for single parents to adopt children or conceive through artificial means? No, of course not.

"Even though we can't always have the ideal situation, we shouldn't be setting up families that *aren't* ideal," the argument then usually becomes. This, of course, is ridiculous as well. The ideal family would have parents who both have steady sources of income and live in a neighborhood that is free of crime and has great public schools; the parents would be fully committed to raising their kids, and so on. But this isn't always the case, and the government certainly doesn't deprive parents that don't fit that picture-perfect paradigm from raising kids.

Further, there is still no scientific evidence that shows kids without a mother figure or a father figure are worse off because of that absence. There are a number of studies—and Rick Santorum likes to cite these a lot—that show a correlation, but none have shown causation. After all, my sister and I—and countless other kids raised by LGBT couples—have turned out just fine. (Or if there is some huge defect, we haven't found it yet and it hasn't been noticed by anyone else, either. Part of the whole nobody-has-realized-independently-that-I-was-raised-by-a-gay-couple thing.) Usually these studies aren't actually identifying a correlation between an absence of a father and poor development; they're identifying a correlation between an impoverished economic situation and poor development. For entirely unrelated reasons, poor families are more likely to be missing a parent. Economic inequality on a pandemic scale is the real problem, not the absence of a mother figure or father figure.

"But wait, you don't really think I'm a radical for believing that all children have the right to both a mother and a father, do you?"

Not any more than you may think I'm a radical for believing that all children have the right to a loving family and a good home. As I spelled out in my testimony, and as I hope I've illustrated in this text, I am of the conviction that love is what makes a family. A family is not defined by who did or did not give birth. A family is not defined by who the biological parents of the children are. A family is not defined by congruence across racial, ethnic, religious, or class lines. A family does not stop being a family when a child goes off to college, gets married, or moves halfway across the world. A family is forever.

"Well, God says that homosexuality is a sin and that marriage is between a man and a woman."

I'd direct you to the First Amendment to the Constitution of the United States, the Treaty of Tripoli, and any number of rulings from the Supreme Court of the United States that have established the freedom of religion in this country. Your god may very well tell you that marriage is only between a man and a woman and that homosexuality is an abomination, but this is not a theocracy. This is a democratic republic, and we have the freedom to worship the god or gods of our choosing and subscribe to our own set of beliefs, so long as those beliefs and that worship don't harm anyone else.

As a number of Christians have pointed out, if the church can push its morality onto the state, the state will certainly inflict its morality onto the church. If Christians attempt to impose the belief that homosexuality is an abomination onto the United States government, they should not be surprised if, at some point in the future, the government tells Christian churches that they are legally bound to marry gay couples, and nobody wants to see religious freedom disregarded in such fashion. Each church has the right to marry the people it deems suitable for marriage. The Catholic Church won't acknowledge my moms' marriage, and if it doesn't want to, that is the church's right. I'm just fine with that. I won't impose my morality on their doctrine if they don't impose theirs on mine. It is better to respect the separation between church and state so wisely established by our Founding Fathers and do unto others as we wish done unto ourselves.